Year of the Lord
Cycle A

Reflections on the Sunday Readings · Rev. Alfred McBride O.Praem.

Religious Education Division
Wm. C. Brown Company Publishers
Dubuque, Iowa

Cover Design
Janet K. Conradi

ISBN 0-697-01847-4

60-1847-01

Contents

Easter/Pentecost

Ordinary Time after Pentecost

Advent

First Sunday of Advent

Isaiah 2: 1-5
In messianic times, nations will stop war.

Roman 13: 11-14
Stop carousing, drunkenness, sexual excess and quarreling.

Matthew 24: 37-44
Be as prepared as a man guarding his house from a thief.

An Advent Choice:
Hedonism or Moral Renewal

Since before Thanksgiving Day the commercial world has already begun the preparation for Christmas. Business concerns itself with financial profits, not the prophets of the coming of Christ. Commerce looks for fiscal, not spiritual, renewal.

Advent summons us to spiritual revitalization. The stores look for monetary salvation. Advent challenges us to seek spiritual salvation. Cash registers ring with economic success. Advent wants to ring bells of moral success. Merchandisers pray for big spenders. The Church of the Advent prays for ethical triumph. Commerce says, "Buy everything we sell." An Advent Church, echoing Christ's words to the rich man, cries "Sell all you have and follow Christ."

We do not lament the enthusiasm of the entrepreneurs. We may regret that Christians may not match and outdo the sharp dedication of the world of business. The challenge to all of us the first Sunday of Advent is to prepare for Christmas, Christ's coming, with us much determination as the children of the world do.

Among other things, this means a question of moral renewal.

Tolstoy's hero in *The Death of Ivan Illich* said, "Maybe I did not live as I ought to have done." Most of us can sympathize with this. We do not tend to throw our hearts into our Christian commitment.

You may recall that when the rock group, The Who, had a concert in Cincinnati, eleven young people died in a stampede to get cheap seats. You may not know that the group follows the motto, "To live is to burn." When interviewed, a member of the group testified, "Rock is going to kill me. Mentally or physically, it's going to get me in the end. It gets everybody in the end." The group is dedicated to absolute emotional release through their music. Not many Christians could say they are committed to absolute personal release through love and service to neighbor.

Millions of people watch the TV show Dallas. The show celebrates materialism. The ranch house might just as well be called the Southfork Hilton. It would take an oil tanker to fill up all the Mercedes in the driveway. Everyone cheats everyone within howdying distance and indulges in an unashamed appeal to the lower emotions. Dallas proves that on TV sex sells . . . and more sex sells better.

The rock group, The Who, and the TV show Dallas, celebrate self-destructive and immoral ways of life. Because they do so with style and contemporary seductiveness, they serve as value shapers for our society.

These are only two of countless examples in our culture where we are numbed into accepting what in Roman times would be called pagan values.

The question before us the first Sunday of Advent is: What will shape our moral values? Will it be the expectation of Christ, or the titillation of the media and business world? What is the use of gaining the approval of an unethical world and losing the integrity of our personhoods? Why eat bread that will turn into stone, rather than the Bread of Life that will be born in Bethlehem (House of Bread)?

Worldly hedonism is making our bodies fat, our hearts weak, our lungs cancerous and our livers white with cirrhosis. Character and discipline, which are essential to being Christian, would give us wholesome lives. We would find interior peace, which is the foundation of external family and political peace.

Respond positively to the Advent challenge or moral and spiritual renewal. Christ is ready to come. The real question is: Are we ready to meet him?

4

Prayer

Father of the Advent, in your mercy you sent
your Son as a savior to be born in Bethlehem, the
House of Bread. Now you continue to send your
Risen Son into our lives, provided we are open
and prepared to receive him. We pledge to you,
in this Advent, that we will begin a process of
moral and spiritual renewal that we may be open
to Christ's coming. Father, give us your love to
make this possible. Amen.

Second Sunday of Advent

Isaiah 11: 1-10
The messiah will be clothed with gifts of the Spirit.

Romans 15: 4-9
Relate to each other in the harmony of the Spirit of Christ.

Matthew 3: 1-12
Jesus will Baptize you in the Spirit.

Turners to the Spirit

There is an old Zen story that tells of a pilgrim who mounted
a horse and traveled over mountain and river to find a wise man
and seek enlightenment. After months of seeking, he found the
wise man and asked him how to be enlightened. The seeker
waited. The wise man said nothing. Finally, growing impatient
with the passing hours, the pilgrim insisted on an answer. The
wise man said, "Why aren't you looking for a horse instead of

enlightenment?" The pilgrim said, "I already have a horse." The wise man smiled, said nothing more, and retreated to his cave.

In a certain sense, this parable is pointless, if one would expect to score a meaning right off. In another sense the story means a lot if one appreciates that it is saying that enlightenment of spiritual insight does not come because one has huffed and puffed to a wise man seeking an easy answer. The Zen parables, with their confusing and enigmatic answers, are saying that spiritual enlightenment comes only after long perseverance and disciplined attention. The upshot of the parable is like a judo of the spirit in which the listener is flipped into a new and unusual consciousness. If it works, then one can begin to travel the ways of the spirit, even though the terrain is unfamiliar and disconcerting.

America today is filled with people seeking enlightenment and spirituality. Some are doing so through the charismatic renewal. Others are "East Turners," that is, attempting to find spirituality in the religions of the Orient. They haven't gone east. They have simply turned east. But whether they happen to be Spirit Turners or East Turners, it is clear they both want a spiritual mode of living.

Today's advent readings are full of Spirit and spirituality talk. Isaiah says that the messiah will be drenched with the gifts of the Spirit. Paul summons us to relate to each other in the harmony of the Spirit of Christ. The Baptist preaches that Christ will baptize us in the Spirit. In each of these three readings, enlightenment is implicit and spirituality is held up as an explicit ideal.

The readings speak of three needs prompting today's spiritual searchings: Religious Authority, Human Friendship, Religious Experience. Spirit Turners and East Turners alike are looking for religious authority. Not so much in the institutional sense, but in the personal sense. They want a moral and spiritual teacher in whom they can believe and trust. Isaiah says: The messiah is just such a person.

The seekers are also looking for simple human friendship. Paul says that this relational harmony comes from a life touched by the Spirit of Jesus. All you have to do is to note the intense fraternity of the Spirit Turners and East Turners to observe their hunger for a friend and a sense of community. The Acts of the Apostles declares that just such communities occurred right after the coming of the Spirit. The need is still here. So also is the response.

Lastly, the searchers want religious experience. They want a real, personal encounter with God, not interrupted by ideas, concepts or any other distraction. They want immediacy with Christ; John baptized with water; Christ baptized with Spirit. That is the religious experience so sought after by the searchers. How well today's worship can respond to that need.

After all, who isn't searching? It's not just the cult people, nor the prayer groups, everyone is searching. Help them, won't you?

Prayer

Father in heaven, help us to be "Spirit Turners."
Move us to seek a proper form of religious
authority, a significant type of human friendship
and a religious experience that opens us to you.
Help us to have a sense of immediacy with
Christ that we may be more than humanistic
"East Turners" and direct our energies to Christ,
the authentic source of our fulfillment. Amen.

Third Sunday of Advent

Isaiah 35: 1-6, 10
Believers meet God with joy and gladness.

James 5: 7-10
Stop worrying. The Lord is at hand.

Matthew 11: 2-11
Tell the Baptist about the joy of the healed.

Humor Is the Secret of Christian Joy

When John Paul II visited Africa, he witnessed a joyous Christianity, a religion meant to be lived and enjoyed. When John the Baptist asks Jesus to prove he is the Messiah (Are you the One?) Jesus does not reply with favorable debate points. Instead he points to the joy of those cured of deafness, leprosy and blindness.

Christianity is the fastest growing religion in Africa. Sundays find village streets empty. Everyone is at Church, enjoying themselves.

Our Advent liturgy begins with the words, "Rejoice in the Lord always." The reading from Isaiah speaks of the redeemed flowing into the house of the Lord, singing and crowned with everlasting joy. The point of all this seems to be: When Christianity is fresh and new and properly understood, it makes people happy. For the Baptist, Jesus used the "proof of joy" as the credential for his messiahship.

African Christians are finding their joy in Christ. This is the first "law of joy." Associated with this is some common sense about attaining joy.

First of all, it is related to humorous contrast. A man on the street with a hat on the side of his head may not seem too funny. But in a Church, a bishop with the miter on the side of his head will cause mirth.

Secondly, in order to be joyful, you should not always be looking for a good time. There will be no fun in life, if everything is supposed to be funny. Mark Jury writes in his book, *Playtime! Americans at Leisure,** that Americans spend 160 billion dollars a year on fun, and this will continue to rise. The fury of such a pursuit is a signal that not much fun is found.

Thirdly, the search for joy is a quest for the infinite. Every joy attracts us because we sense there will be yet a more boundless pleasure. No one thing or person seems to satisfy us, because we

---

*Mark Jury, *Playtime! Americans at Leisure*, New York: Harcourt Brace Jovanovich, 1977.

notice we have an appetite for everything. A man may have met the woman of his dreams one year, yet his eyes stray to another sometimes in the next year. The joy of a great party at night often yields to the next day's hangover. No one element can satisfy us, only the infinite.

This Infinite is God, Father, Jesus, Spirit.

Perhaps one of the best methods for seeking joy is to have a sense of Divine Humor. In order to laugh at a joke, we must be able to "see the point." We say that people have no sense of humor because they never see the point. God has made the world in such a way that He is the point of everything we see. The world around us is a window through which we may see God. Mountains tell us of His power and snowflakes of His purity. The poor, hungry and naked are Christ in disguise. The "point" of creation is the Creator.

All sins are "missing the point." (The Hebrew word for sin means *missing the mark*.) Sinners grab things as ends in themselves, instead of roads to God. Sinners are too solemn about this world. It is too important to them. So they miss the point, and therefore miss the God who could make them really happy. Many of today's most honored playwrights and moviemakers are terribly solemn. The genius of their skills conceals a despair flowing from their cramped hearts.

Christians are meant to be humorous and lighthearted. That way they have a better chance of getting the whole point of creation. They can smile because they know how to cry. They can laugh because they know how to suffer. They can see God because they get the whole point of it all.

Prayer

Father of happiness, awaken in us every day the
humorous sense we need to see the whole point
of the universe. Give us wit with our worldly
wisdom so that we are open to the joyful
surprises you constantly prepare for us. Rescue
us from solemnity and move us to a good humor
that our joy may be pure and growing. Amen.

Fourth Sunday of Advent

Isaiah 7: 10-14
A virgin will give birth to Emmanuel.

Romans 1: 1-7
Jesus is born of the House of David.

Matthew 1: 18-24
Joseph realizes Jesus will be born of the Holy Spirit.

Virginal Mary-Celibate Joseph, a Celebration of Love

A young Catholic boy from a Catholic school was telling a university professor who lived next door about the Blessed Mother. The professor made fun of the boy by saying, "There is no difference between her and my mother." With just as nimble a wit, the boy replied, "That's what you think. But there's a heck of a lot of difference between the sons."

And yet there is a unique difference between the mothers, for Mary is a virgin mother. Some women are virgins because they never had a chance to marry. Other women are virgins because they simply chose not to marry. A third group of women are virgins because they made a vow to God not to marry. Mary belongs to this third group.

How do we know that Mary vowed virginity to God? It is implied in the answer Mary gave to the Angel Gabriel at the Annunciation. The angel told her she would give birth to a son. Mary did not say, "I am not going to get married, therefore I would not have a baby." Nor did she say, "I don't want a husband, so how can this come about." In fact she is already betrothed to Joseph. Legally she was bound to marry him.

She says, "How can this be, since I know not man." The word *know* here is the biblical word for sexual union. She knew she would be married, and therefore under normal circumstances

10

would anticipate sexual union with her husband. We infer from her words that she and Joseph had agreed to a marriage in which she would remain a virgin and he would remain a celibate.

The angel assures her that she will conceive by the power of the Holy Spirit. Divine love will supplant human love in the generation of her son.

Matthew brings out the same message in the account of Joseph's dilemma. He found out that his forthcoming wife was pregnant. What had brought this about? He knew she had vowed virginity as he had pledged celibacy. Joseph had kept his vow and therefore was deeply disturbed by the possibility that Mary had not kept hers. He immediately began thinking of divorce proceedings. (Technically, a betrothal was legally considered a marriage, even though the couple did not live together.)

An angel appears to Joseph to reassure him that the child would be born by the power of the Holy Spirit. "Joseph, have no fear about taking Mary as your wife. It is by the Holy Spirit that she has conceived the child."

Many who have reflected on this scene have wondered: Was Joseph old or young? Pious tradition and art like to portray him as an old man. The assumption is that he could more easily be celibate due to his age than to his virtue presenting a kind of "pious front" for this mysterious event.

But in order for Joseph to be a saint, it is more reasonable to suppose he was a young man, strong and virile. This would make his celibate discipline a voluntary promise more worthy of admiration. Moreover, Jewish custom frowned on June-December marriages. Their practices disapproved of what Shakespeare calls the union of "crabbed age and youth." The Talmud approved of such marriages only in the case of widows and widowers.

Joseph was a young man married to a young woman. They kept between them a precious secret, wrapped in a love characterized by joy and sacrifice. As natural mother and foster father, Mary and Joseph nourished and reared the most wondrous son in history. Blessed be this marvelous couple for their faith, obedience and insight. In celebrating their love we best prepare for the Christmas feast that is upon us.

Prayer

Praise to you, Holy Spirit, who did conceive
Jesus in the womb of the Virgin Mary by your
divine power of love. Instill in us the proper
sense of reverence, awe and wonder that should
characterize our genuine faith response to this
mystery. May we be inspired by the sacrificial
love displayed by the vows of virginity and
celibacy in the lives of Mary and Joseph. May
such love dedication affect all our lives. Amen.

Christmas

Christmas Day

Isaiah 9: 1-6
They named the child Wonder-Counselor, God-Hero.

Titus 2: 11-14
The grace of God has appeared in Jesus.

Luke 2: 1-14
Jesus is messiah and Lord.

The God in the Cave

If the findings of our archaeologists be correct, the first humans were cave people. Science tells us humanity began in a cave. Christian faith teaches that humanity is born again in a cave. In the cave-stable of Bethlehem, the mystery of the Incarnation occurs. The God-man is born. As the cave men [and women] were the origin of the old humanity, Jesus is the origin of the new humanity. The critical difference between the two is that the second one was a God marvelously and mysteriously united to humanity.

The scene at the cave is one full of startling contrasts. The God who made the universe now has hands too small to touch the heads of the cattle. The God whose independence was infinite now must look to his mother's milk for survival. The God whose power made the heat of the sun will feel a chill unless warmed by the swaddling clothes and the warm breath of the animals. Infinite power has become vulnerability. Absolute freedom has assumed the annoyances of limitation. The dazzling light of divine glory has accepted the shadows imposed by the night.

The central secret of the Christmas story is to be found in these amazing contrasts. To forget the God in the cave is to reduce the Bethlehem event to a charming birth scene with no special meaning. Yet, to see only the God would endow the setting with an aura of magic and myth and rob it of any historical impact. Christmas is destroyed when the contrast is ignored or denied.

In our humanistic times there is an intolerance for letting the divine have any effective presence or action in human fulfillment. We are very much like the deists of the eighteenth century who admitted the existence of God, but believed He left us to run everything ourselves. This becomes a practical atheism since it denies God's action in life just as much as an unbeliever would. In celebrating Christmas we must push beyond humanism and with faith acknowledge the God in the cave.

The humanists admire the child. The shepherds and kings adore him. Humanists will sing nursery rhymes. Angels sing, "Glory to God in high heaven." Unbelievers will just rock the cradle. Believers will let the cradle rock the world. The proud who know everything will miss the point of Christmas. The humble who know that they don't know everything will find the living truth in Jesus, the Savior. The strong, who believe power is the ultimate goal, will deny this vulnerability of a God-child. The put-upon, the suffering, the poor, the desperate, the disturbed will take new heart in knowing that they can be healed by One who accepts and purifies their experience.

The ancient Romans built a pantheon for all the gods of the world. They asked the Christians to put Jesus in with the other gods. "Be open minded. Join the brotherhood of world religions." The Christians said no thanks, if it meant that Jesus would be robbed of the uniqueness of his true divinity. Today's humanists wants to build a pantheon for the world's great men. Again the Christians are asked to enshrine Jesus as the Great Moral Teacher, as though he were among equals. Again the Christian response must be a firm and loving no. Jesus is the God-man and savior.

As we join the shepherds in this feast of Light, let us sing of our faith in the God-man in the cave, and agree, as he did, to accept the values of vulnerability, dependence and limitation as our starting point for healing, loving and freedom seeking. Pray to Mary these words: "O hold him tenderly, dear mother. For he is a kingdom in the hearts of men."

Prayer

O Christ Jesus, at once human and divine, we stand with reverence in the face of so profound a mystery. We admire you as child. We adore you as God. We thank you for the splendid Christmas present of the Incarnation. With the shepherds we try to make a humble act of faith in your total reality. With the angels we sing of your glory. With your help we will try to love as you wish us to do. Glory to you in high heaven and great peace to all of us on earth. Amen.

Feast of the Holy Family

Sirach 3: 2-6, 12-14
The value of revering parents.

Colossians 3: 12-21
The value of respect between the spouses.

Matthew 2: 13-15, 19-23
The value of parental concern for children.

Fidelity in the Family Is Essential

This feast of the Holy Family draws our attention to the state of family life in America today. Opinions about family life vary widely.

Ferdinand Lundberg states that the family is dead except for the first two years of child raising. Pessimists say the family is racing to oblivion.

But family optimists claim that the family is in for a Golden Age. As leisure spreads the family will spend more time together. They will derive satisfaction from joint activity. Moreover, the very instability of the times will make people turn to the family for stability. In this view, the family is a giant shock absorber. It is the place where the battered individual returns after doing battle with the world.

One thing is certain: The family is by no means dead. Despite a mounting divorce rate, sixty percent of all families remain intact. One reason that accounts for the statistics about soaring divorce rates, is the number of third and fourth marriages among those in the forty percent who get divorced in the first place.

It is unfortunate that more attention seems to be given to divorce than to stability in marriage. The prevalence of acceptance of divorce as a matter of fact makes marital fidelity more difficult, because it causes couples to think fidelity may not be possible or desirable. We hear of "no fault" divorce. Legally, there may be some merit in this. But morally the concept is a disaster because it induces the idea that one has no ethical responsibility to keep one's promises.

We hear of "civilized divorce." Suzanne Jordan writes, "This is like controlled, mature adults spanking their children after they have cooled off. I think people should be upset about so serious a thing as divorce."

The Holy Family succeeded because the members were bound to one another by a love rooted in God. Their fidelity to each other reflected the everlasting fidelity of the divine. They of all people knew that God kept His promises to the human race. Hence they realized that promises could be kept. They could observe the model of good promise keeping and they also, in prayer, experienced the inner mystical power of God who made sure that promises would be honored.

If today's families looked only to the world for their signals, they would get the idea that promises can never be anything more than temporary. But if more families attended to the example of the Holy Family on earth and the Holy Trinity in heaven, they might be more inspired to realize that fidelity is achievable.

The Church calls families to be in a sacramental union that witnesses to the world how Christ and the Church unite in a shared value system. A sacrament is an awareness provoker, revealing the divine reality underneath the external signs. Families need to be committed to a shared value ideal.

An old Beatles' song has these lines, "When in times of trouble, Mother Mary comes to me, singing songs of comfort, Let it Be, Let it Be." Families, who learn about unconditioned loving of each other can echo this song: "Let there be being. Let there be love. Let there be fidelity." In singing out this canticle, families will resonate with the God of Genesis as Creator, proclaiming, "Let there be vitality and faithfulness."

There is too much talk about the death of love in marriage. We should replace this with more talk about the birth of love in prayer and fidelity. The Holy Family is ready to pray with us. Beginning with prayer and ending in action, all of our families will be holy and stable as well.

Prayer

Holy Trinity, divine example of communal love
and fidelity, enable our Christian families to
come to firm and faithful cohesion in love. We
praise you for the gift of the example of the Holy
Family of Jesus, Mary and Joseph. May we see a
new flowering of family life in these troubled
times. This we ask in union with the prayers of
the Holy Family of Nazareth. Amen.

Solemnity of Mary, the Mother of God

Numbers 6: 22-27
The Great Blessing.

Galatians 4: 4-7
God blessed us in his Son, born of a woman.

Luke 2: 16-21
The shepherds understood the blessing of Jesus born of Mary.

God's Mother—The Total and Feminine Woman

One of the surest ways of starting an argument is to take a stand on the meaning of being a woman today. The American woman is not likely to agree with these words of Katherine in *The Taming of the Shrew:*

> *"I am ashamed that women are so simple*
> *To offer war where they should kneel for peace*
> *Or seek for rule, supremacy and sway*
> *When they are bound to serve, love and obey."*

Well, then what should be the role of woman? The liberation movement has generated two schools of thought, one characterized by the feminists, the other, by the total woman advocates. The feminists fight the exploitation of women with help from the pill, legal abortion, equal rights laws and a fair share of the job market. The Total Woman contingent pleads for monogamy, pleasure in taking care of home and children, religious faith, poise and self-confidence. One group stresses self-fulfillment outside the home. The other emphasizes self-realization inside the home. Both claim to be against a discrimination that would ignore women's minds and waste their talents.

As in any passionate movement for rights, there are bound to be exaggerations with which one would disagree. Generally speaking, the goals are good. The quarrel abides about some of the means. This is not the place nor the agency to settle the debate. But it is a place to take some light from the story of Mary, the Virgin Mother of God.

On this New Year's Day, we celebrate the feast of the Solemnity of Mary as Mother of God. No other woman in history was so self-fulfilled, for she was filled with God, the only One who can absolutely fill the human heart. In a sermon on Mary, Martin Luther once said, "We have crowded all her glory into a single word, Mother of God. No one can say anything greater of her to her, though he had as many tongues as the leaves on the tree, the stars in the sky or the sands by the seas."

The concentration on self-realization today is on what we can do to improve ourselves. Mary put her mind on what God could do to improve her life. As she sang, "He who is mighty has done great things for me." Now there is nothing wrong in using one's own talents to the full and trying to develop them. In fact, it is our duty to take our gifts and use them to the full. The mistake comes from believing that only our own energies and input are needed.

The key to this dilemma is found in the distinction between preparation and production. Human energy and imagination prepares us for fulfillment. It stirs in us the thirst for the need for total completion. It is God who produces the fulfillment, if we are open to the Lord in faith. Why is there an ache, an emptiness and a void in so many apparently fulfilled people? Why do the rich and the famous go on thirsting, hungering and searching? It is because they mistook the preparation for the product.

Mary was prepared for the conception of Jesus. She was a woman of faith and prayer. And one day she was "surprised by joy" to have her whole being filled with God. The Wood of the Cross was prepared for the victim, but Jesus was the fulfiller. The body-person of Mary was prepared. God was the fulfiller. We admire and honor today's search for realization by both women and men. The point is to see that this is only a preparation—a necessary one indeed—for the genuine fulfillment that comes from God. He, who is mighty, will do great things for us, too.

Prayer

O Mary, it is totally fitting to bless you, the birth-giver of God. You are ever blessed and undefiled. As mother of God you are more honorabale than the angels. You are beyond compare and more glorious than the seraphim. You have borne God the Word. Birth-giver of God, we magnify you to all the world. Amen. (This is a hymn to Mary sung after the consecration in the divine liturgy of St. John Chrysostom.)

Epiphany

Isaiah 60: 1-6
The Lord is the light of thinking persons.

Ephesians 3: 2-3, 5-6
A ministry of preaching requires learning and prayer.

Matthew 2: 1-12
Thinking men sought the Lord.

Three Thoughtful Persons

So much is said today about our emotional thirst for God that we could forget there is a mental drive to the Lord as well. The peril implicit in dwelling only on the religion of the heart is that God becomes a sentimental object. Seen this way, God is used for selfish reasons. We call on God to stroke our feelings whenever we feel bad. The result is that we mask our self-indulgence under a spiritual veneer. It's okay to spend our time licking our wounds—or have God caress them for us. This is but another tricky form of egoism reinforced by sentimental religion.

But all feeling and no thinking makes religion not only dull but untrue. Of course, the opposite is equally destructive. The religion of intellect alone would yield cold pride. This makes the possessor imagine he or she has created God. What is needed is the total person of faith with a faith that feeds on both the feelings of the heart and the thinking powers of the mind. If there is an excess today, it is the exaggeration of feeling at the expense of thinking. Religion needs a mighty infusion of thinking people.

Our feast of the Epiphany tells the story of the manifestation of the glory of God in Christ. It is the celebration of Christ's divinity. It is also the narrative of three thoughtful men, the Magi, whose inquiring minds brought them to seek God. Yes, their hearts persuaded them to reach for God but they used the strategies of their minds to plot the route. They put their minds at the service of faith and were not disappointed.

To raise one's voice in praise of thinking people is like talking into the wind. The gales of emotion, vague mysticism, psychic writhings and other unleashed passions have little patience with the sober act of thinking. No matter. A plea for wise men, like the Magi, who honor the act and art of thought must be trumpeted despite the opposition. A world without solid thought is prey to barbarism. A religion without intellect is a tinder box for fanaticism. We must balance the ocean of the heart with the sky of the mind—the emotions of the heart with the passions of the mind.

In accepting the Nobel prize for literature, novelist Saul Bellow addressed the members of the Swedish academy with these words: "The writer must begin to use his intelligence—long unused. He must begin to think. How great today's writers would be if they recognized there is an immense desire to return to what is simple and true. To what is fundamental, enduring and essential."

His wise words apply just as well to Christian believers. Epiphany calls us to be people of wisdom. That is not going to happen without the use of our brains. God gave us minds and expects us to exercise them. It is all well and good to extol simple faith, but we live in complex and confusing times. The challenge to believers is to analyze, sort out and critique the meaning of society, politics, sex, and other topics competing for our attention and commitment.

Catholic tradition abounds with countless examples of thoughtful, wise people: Augustine, Aquinas, Thomas More. Even the mystical Teresa of Avila stood squarely for the dignity of the mind. On this "Thinking Man's" feast of Epiphany stir up your minds as well as your hearts. A thought-less world needs you.

Prayer

Spirit of wisdom, put some fire in our minds.
Motivate us to use our intellects both to search
for God and to help explain the meaning of God
in human life. Show us the attractiveness of the
quest for wisdom and curb our desire to
eliminate the intelligence in the act of faith.
Infuse our resolve to imitate the example of the
Magi whose faith filled, loving—mental
inquiry—led them to adore the Christ. We praise
you, most Holy Spirit. Amen.

Feast of the Baptism of Our Lord

Isaiah 42: 1-4; 6-7
God anoints His servant to ministry of justice.

Acts 10: 34-38
Peter brings Cornelius "the good news of peace."

Matthew 3: 13-17
Jesus is anointed for his justice ministry.

Of Rivers and Preachers

Preparing for the Second Vatican Council, Pope John XXIII sent out a call for Church renewal from the banks of the Tiber. When Martin Luther King wanted to call America to act on Civil Rights for Blacks he raised his voice by the banks of the Potomac and stirred 250,000 listeners with his words, "I have a dream." By the banks of the Thames, Winston Churchill thrilled the hearts of the British with his challenge to "blood, sweat and tears."

The Jews in exile had wept by the banks of the "waters of Babylon" and cried out for freedom. Ezechiel stood by those waters and called them to a faith that would bring their restoration to Israel. In American colonial times, Jesuit missionaries roamed the waters of the Mississippi calling the Indians to salvation in Christ. The combination of water images and prophetic calls to spiritual renewal abound in history and are set before us in the fiery sermons of John the Baptist at the banks of the Jordan.

The appearance of Jesus at Jordan's banks culminates the baptismal and preaching scenes. Jesus needs no repentance for he is sinless, yet as the humble servant of the Father, he comes to the Jordan, not to be washed from sin, but to be anointed Messiah. The scene combines the creation story of Genesis with the Servant Songs of Isaiah about the mission and ministry of the Messiah.

One is reminded of the creation story by the dove and the river. In Genesis, creation is brought about by the power of God's Breath (or Spirit) who draws life from the watery chaos. This Breath-Spirit of God hovers over the chaos like a dove. The Jordan is the new watery chaos over which the dove/Spirit of God hovers to begin a new creation in Jesus.

The scene also recalls the first of the Servant Songs of Isaiah:

> Here is my servant whom I uphold,
> my chosen one with whom I am pleased
> Upon whom I have put my spirit;
> He shall bring forth justice to the nations.—Isaish 42: 1–4

> This is my beloved Son.
> May favor rests on him.—Matthew 3: 17

At the Jordan, Jesus brings to full meaning the message of the Baptist. Jesus will make the dreams of the poor and humble come true. The best news of all is that he will both bring justice and make people just. Through his passion and resurrection, Jesus will release people from the heavy burden of guilt and anxiety resulting from sin. The saving work of Jesus will give people an awareness of being just. Not a self-righteous justice born of false piety, but a humble and honest justice flowing from God.

In this Church the waters of the Jordan flow at our Baptismal font. On the day of our baptism we were freed from sin's domination by the power of the Dove/Spirit who hovered over us and then moved deeply into our hearts, drawing us from the chaos and disorder of our passions and unruly desires. Having become a new creation in Christ, we then are given the mission and ministry to seek justice and love all people whom we meet.

In this service of the word, we echo the call to renewal as John did by the Jordan banks. We continue the process of purification from sin through the Rite of Reconciliation. There is no need for either moral guilt nor psychological anxiety to paralyze us. We need to be free to serve. We were made free, let us stay that way.

Prayer

Father in heaven, you anointed your Son at the
Jordan to go forth on a mission and ministry of
justice. We too have been anointed in our own
baptisms for a similar mission to act justly and
bring justice to those suffering from both the
symptoms and causes of injustice. Fulfill within
us the high potential of our baptismal calling
that the world may celebrate justice with joy.
Amen.

Ordinary Time after Christmas

Second Sunday
of Ordinary Time

Isaiah 49: 3, 5-6
The Lamb symbolizes the life of God's Servant.

1 Corinthians 1: 1-3
God calls all of us to be holy.

John 1: 29-34
Behold God's lamb who accepts death, even a violent one.

The Value of Facing and Accepting Death

The hardest thing in life is the willingness to accept one's death. Freud says most people deny death by thinking they are immortal. Yet the capacity to face up to one's death releases moral courage and spiritual insight.

Joan of Arc came to terms with death and did not flinch when the prospect of burning at the stake lay before her. The results were dramatic. An ignorant, uneducated woman sounded wiser than the theologians who grilled her. When the Inquisitor asked her, "Joan, are you in the state of grace?" she replied: "If I am, may the Lord keep me there. If I am not, may the Lord put me there."

Death is the darkest and most mysterious reality we must all face. If we face it with courage and acceptance, not just when it is imminent but early in our lives, we are usually moved to be more courageous and wise. This is even truer when we may face the prospect of dying violently as a martyr. Such is the meaning of applying the term *Lamb of God* to Jesus in the Gospel.

In a shepherd culture such as that of the Jews, the lamb was both a centerpiece of the economy as well as of their religion. Flocks of lambs spelled money and prosperity for shepherds. But lambs also were designated for death by the knife for religious purposes. The lamb symbolized innocence.

31

Secondly, the lamb did not resist death, but lay willingly there as the ceremonial killing took place. (That is why it is hard to kill a lamb.) Using human projection, the lamb seems to know it is destined for death, willingly accepts it and faces death despite the violence.

The martyred animal stood for the ideal of human martyrdom in which the human person wills death by acceptance for a special purpose. Furthermore the Lamb symbolized immortality, for when the fire converted the body of the lamb into the smoke that rose to the skies, it is lovingly taken into the bosom of God. So when a person imitates the lamb, according to scripture, by accepting death, facing it bravely even when it means martyrdom, the person creates in others a sense of freedom from both the fear of death and the burden of sin which is spiritual death.

John the Baptist says, "Behold the Lamb of God who takes away the sin of the world." He is saying, "Behold the innocent man who does not deny death, who faces it with acceptance, even a violent death—to liberate us from the fear of death and the weight of sin." On Mount Moriah, Abraham asked God, "Where is the lamb who will replace my son on this rock of sacrifice?" Centuries later God answers through the lips of the Baptist at the Jordan. "Here is the lamb, Jesus Christ."

What is the motivation in the lamb symbol? Lambs, as animals, have no capacity for motivation except in terms of instincts for sex and food. The human-lamb-martyr is moved by love. Those who have coped with death know how to love, for they come to know that "love conquers all," even death and sin. Since all great love demands sacrifice, this person is willing to die for love. Someone once said, "If it's yours be willing to die for it. If not, keep your hands off it."

Some claim it is morbid to think of death. That is true if one dwells on the physical details and not on the purification of one's attitudes in the face of death—dread, fear, recoil. To look at death meaningfully is to look at one's attitude toward it and move from denial to acceptance.

This is a process that unlocks love and courage. Look into the eyes of Jesus the Lamb. See his acceptance and sense of purpose. Now look in your own heart. Test your own acceptance, love and courage. Then turn back to Christ for more than an example. He has the love power to draw you into the purity of his own attitudes.

Prayer

Holy Spirit whose loving insight can help us come to terms with our physical death and our moral death in sin, guide us to face death with acceptance, thus overcoming denial of death. Unite us to the attitudes of Jesus the Lamb, the innocent man/martyr freeing us from the fear of physical death and the spiritual death of sin. Thus may we be born again in love and courage. Amen.

Third Sunday of Ordinary Time

Isaiah 8: 23; 9: 3
People in darkness look for the light of saving leaders.

1 Corinthians 1: 10-13, 17
Lead people out of factions and quarrels.

Matthew 4: 12-23
Jesus picks leaders like Peter for the Church.

Jesus Calls Peter as a Disciple and Leader

In today's gospel we celebrate Christ's calling Peter to be an apostle.

Son of Jona (Bar-Jona) and brother of Andrew, Peter followed the fisherman profession of his family. It was Andrew who introduced Peter to Jesus. We know more about Peter than any of the other apostles, for he is mentioned 190 times in the New Testament, as contrasted with 130 references to all the other apostles.

Jesus picked a leader when he chose Peter. And Peter acted like a leader. He acts as spokesman for the apostles, asking the meaning of puzzling parables and correctly identifying Jesus as Messiah and Son of God. Jesus preaches from Peter's boat and often stays at Peter's house. Jesus places the leadership of the Church in Peter's hands and reconfirms this at the Last Supper. "But I have prayed for you that your faith may never fail. You in turn must strengthen your brothers." (Luke 22: 32)

Peter always seems to be "first." He was first to see the Risen Lord, first to preach the Gospel after Pentecost and first disciple to perform a miracle. He baptizes the first gentile convert, Cornelius, and he was first to defend Christ and Christians before a hostile Sanhedrin.

Leadership images surround him: the Christian Fisherman, the Shepherd Christ calls to feed the lambs, Receiver of special revelation on the mount of the Transfiguration, Confessor of true faith at Caesarea Phillipi, Guardian against false teaching. (Cf. 2 Peter 1: 20–21)

All this leadership talk focuses on the fact of a Petrine Ministry in the New Testament Church. It shows that Jesus wanted one person who would serve as minister to the whole Christian community. Such a minister-leader works together with and listens to and consults with others as did Peter.

Peter is a most appealing human leader—impulsive, inadequate, faltering, yet able to repent. He wanted to walk on water, but he sank into the waves and screamed in fear, he a man of the sea. This is no invincible leader, unable to share his anxiety.

He stares at the glory of the transfiguration and distractedly thinks of "housing" for the three figures.

Remorselessly practical, he wants a body count on how often he should be charitable. Peter vows to stand by Jesus and drink the cup of pain. Instead he falls asleep at the crucial hour and is so nervous at Christ's arrest that he cravenly denies him.

In the "denial scene" we see a Peter not yet strong enough to lead. In the "repentance scene" we watch a grown man cry and show that he is big enough to admit he was wrong. Now he is strong enough to lead. At Caesarea Phillipi Jesus asked Peter, "Do you understand me?" Peter did and was made the rock of the Church.

At the Easter scene in Galilee, Jesus asked Peter, "Do you love me?" Peter said yes and was made the nourisher of the lambs, of people. Peter displayed faith-informed, mental sharpness in the first case and warm love in the second, characteristics of a true leader.

This leadership in faith and love forms the twin poles of the Petrine Ministry. It is an example for all of us who have a leadership call in the Christian community as parents, teachers, enablers, neighbors and friends.

John Paul II ministers to the whole Church. Each of us ministers to our small part of the Church. All of us must believe and love to be true leaders . . . And be human enough to admit our faults and grow.

Prayer

Jesus, the caller to discipleship and leadership, touch us with the questions that will bring forth our faith and love. Challenge us again with the questions you put to Peter: "Will you follow me? Do you understand me? Do you love me?" With your grace we shall give positive assent to these questions, as did Peter. We praise you Lord for the Petrine Ministry in the Church. Amen.

Fourth Sunday
of Ordinary Time

Zephaniah 2: 3; 3: 12-13
Seek the values of justice, humility and truth.

1 Corinthians 1: 26-31
God chooses the "absurd" to shame the wise.

Matthew 5: 1-12
The charter for Christian happiness.

Beatitudes: Profile for Christian Living

The beatitudes constitute Christ's plan for a happy person.
Our narcissistic culture has a different plan. Christopher
Lasch, in his book, *The Culture of Narcissus,* draws an example of
a plan for happiness from secular life. He cites one time radical
Jerry Rubin.

> In his coyly titled memoir, *Growing (Up) at
> Thirty Seven,** Rubin testifies to the salutary effect
> of his health regimen. After years of neglect he
> gave himself permission to be healthy and
> quickly lost thirty pounds. Health foods, jogging,
> yoga, sauna baths, chiropractors and
> acupuncturists made him feel at thirty seven, like
> twenty five. He shed his protective armor, his
> sexism, his addiction to love and learned "to love
> myself so that I do not need another to be

---

*Rubin, Jerry, *Growing (Up) at Thirty Seven,* New York: M. Evans, 1976.

happy. . . ." Rubin discusses the "female in me," the need for a more tolerant view of homosexuality and the need "to make peace with his parents" as if these commonplaces represented hard won insights into the human condition. . . . Like many ex-radicals he has succeeded only in exchanging current therapeutic slogans for the political slogans he used to mouth with equal disregard for their content.*

The eight beatitudes of the world are:

Blessed are the rich, they must be doing something right.

Blessed are the powerful, for might makes right.

Blessed are the hedonists, for pleasure is the measure of man.

Blessed are the ambitious, for when push comes to shove, they walk right over you.

Blessed are the sinful, for they have more fun.

Blessed are the warmakers, for they make a lot of money.

Blessed are the pornographers, they save us from the trouble of loving.

Blessed are the oppressors, they keep the poor in poverty and give us more of the pie.

The beatitudes of Christ must be read against the world's beatitudes. Jesus climbed a hill at Galilee to preach the beatitudes. He later ascended the hill of Calvary to practice them. His point: One must die to the world's values. His second point: The world may kill you for refusing to live by its values. The world's beatitudes work for the rich, the powerful, the beautiful people, so long as they can keep one billion people poor and hungry, so long as they can brutalize the majority to safeguard the hedonism of a minority.

---

*Lasch, Christopher, *The Culture of Narcissus*, New York: Warner, 1979, pages 44–46.

The self-indulgence of a few who practice the world's beatitudes is purchased by the suppression of the many. Christ warns the powerful about their folly. Christ cautions the weak not to look longingly at the beatitudes of the mighty.

To all people he preaches: Depend on God, not money. Use soul force against the power tactics of the mighty. Face up to and mourn the sense of the tragic and empathize with those who suffer. Hunger for the permanence of holiness rather than fleeting fame. Concentrate on the forgiveness of sin, not its justification. Make peace to crowd out war. Surround sex with love that no one be exploited. Don't be afraid to suffer in the fight for justice.

This marvelous charter of the Christian covenant is one of the most powerful such statements found in the Scripture. The eight values contained therein establish a profile of what it means to be a Christian: The world's beatitudes lead to sin and death. Christ's lead to love and eternal happiness. Make your choice for Christ.

Prayer

Father of us all, draw us to internalize the eight values taught by Jesus on the Mount of the Beatitudes. Relieve us from the illusions of the world that would draw us into sin, hedonism and insensitivity to the poor. Create in our hearts the space for the Christian values that will make our lives worthwhile. For this we pray in Christ and the Spirit. Amen.

Fifth Sunday of Ordinary Time

Isaiah 58: 7-10
Your "spiritual" light shall shine like the dawn.

1 Corinthians 2: 1-5
The conviction in your witness is from the Spirit.

Matthew 5: 13-16
You are the "spiritual" light and city to be seen.

Self and Spirit—Who Shines?

It used to be said that God helps those who help themselves. But the prevailing wisdom today is: There is no help from God. You can only help yourself. The market place rings with the teachings about self-help. A few years ago their gospel was the buildup of self through inner awareness, the wisdom of Guru X, the techniques of system Y and the mantras of meditation Z.

The tune has changed. Away with the passive repose of inner searches. Bring on the assertive therapies. Since people are trying to push you around, the best thing you can do is to push them first. While this approach may help some excessively timid and bashful souls, it is most likely just another way for bullies to improve on their techniques and justify their boorish behavior.

What is the substance of the new self-help teachings? Personal happiness and success is the most important thing in life. Other people's desires, rights and values are important only if they help me. Nothing I do is wrong unless it makes me unhappy. Guilt is a purely subjective feeling. Guilt is always bad and should not be considered a useful response to any results of my behavior. I should only get involved in worthwhile causes when they enhance my success and happiness. As one of these promoters put it: "By the time you accept my teaching, you will have fallen in love with a very special person . . . you!"

Now, no one will quibble about the need to love, respect and reverence one's self. Jesus tells us that we are to love others as we love ourselves. Jesus was also insistent in tying this advice to a loving trust in God. He knew that once we eliminate the divine dimension from the story, we are doomed to be an egotistic self-helper. It's all very commercial. Push pays off. The end result, however, is tragic, both for the pusher and the pushee. The selfishly assertive wind up lonely since the only one they cared about was themselves. The ones they wounded are equally lonely, looking for someone to help them.

Today's readings state clearly that the spiritual horizon is critical for human fulfillment. Self-help without God sheds nothing but darkness. Linked to the Lord, the self will shed a "spiritual" light as cheerful as the dawn. Paul says that he refuses a human wisdom without the Cross. He found that in the mystery of the Cross, the Spirit endowed the human with the conviction and energy needed to love others. Jesus tells the people of faith that they will be the salt of the earth, the city on the hill and the light to be seen. Such people are signs of encouragement to the world, not symbols of self-enclosed bitterness.

The drift of the helping experience runs in cycles. Sometimes the mood is all divine. Let God do it. In other periods, such as our own, the theme is totally human. Let me do it. History is a record of these shifts from exaggerated dependence on God to excessive dependence on self. Those who throw themselves on God, while doing nothing for themselves, desire a divine welfare state. Those who shift only for themselves produce a state of moral anarchy. The only correct way is produced by the tension between faith reliance on God and human reliance on self. When the two mesh with some grace and poise, the kingdom of God and human happiness can really occur. It's always a hard won lesson, but one that can indeed be learned.

Prayer

Lord Jesus, eminent Helper of all who need you, keep before us the total picture in the helping experience. We realize we have a duty to help ourselves. May we not forget that your divine aid is also a needed part of self-development and love of others. Persuade us to bear the part of self-development and love of other. Persuade us to bear the Cross which is the essence of this tension. We look to our own powers. We also look to yours. With both we can reach fulfillment. Amen.

Sixth Sunday of Ordinary Time

Sirach 15: 15-20
To keep the commandments is to be lovingly loyal to God.

1 Corinthians 2: 6-10
God's wisdom is the inner content of the commandments.

Matthew 5: 17-37
You have heard the Law. But you should know its meaning.

The Meaning and Purpose of God's Laws

When St. Teresa of Avila entered the Incarnation convent as a lively eighteen-year-old woman, she found a pleasant group of nuns. Most of them were middle-class women from Avila and the surrounding area.

They loved to talk, laugh, tell stories, take trips and visit often with their friends and relatives. They were not strictly faithful to the ancient rule of Carmel. They were willing to do the basic prayer hours and some other spiritual obligations, but on the whole they were little more than a congenial group of women. They had little interest in fasting, contemplation, social concern or other deeper aspects of the Carmelite vocation. They paid lip service to only the barest minimum of the classical Rule of Carmel.

Teresa was herself a fun loving, gregarious Spanish woman. She thoroughly enjoyed life at the Incarnation, with one difference. She thought something was wrong. And the more she thought about it, the more convinced she was that the Carmelite vocation was something more than living a gently self-indulgent life. No one was sinning. Sin did not abound.

But on the other hand, no one was soaring in contemplation. Grace did not abound either. In a twenty-year-long search for the essential spirit of the Carmelite Rule, Teresa found the secret and began a reform of the Carmel that for over four centuries has been one of the most successful recoveries of the spirit of the Gospel in the history of the Church.

The secret that Teresa found was that the spirit of the Rule deserves as much attention as its exterior observance. And that when one abandons the interior spirit, it won't be long before the exterior conformity begins to wane as well.

The Gospel reading deals with Religious Law. Jesus notes that people tend to observe the externals of the Law of God, with little appreciation of its interior purpose and meaning. How often today he says, *"You have heard . . . but. . . ."*

People hear the words of the Law, but they do not appreciate the reasons. The ultimate reasons for God's Law are (1) to stop us from harming persons; (2) to create a proper internal attitude toward God and People; (3) to bring us to a love that unites our inner intentions with our outer behavior.

To stop us from harming persons. God's laws about sex are meant to keep us from exploiting bodies as though there were no person involved. God's laws about abusive language and lies are meant to keep us from ruining reputations and destroying people's self-respect. God's laws about killing are meant to help us respect life.

To create a proper attitude to God and people. Not only is it wrong to do a sin, it is also wrong to plan a sin. Jesus does not wait for the evil tree to bear fruit. He is against the very sowing of the evil seed by thinking about it and planning. We must work just as hard on our attitudes as we do on our behavior.

To bring us to love. The final purpose of God's law is to teach us how to love. Love is always a unitive force. It begins with ourselves when it unites our inner attitudes with outer actions. Love makes us a together person. Love pulls together all our competing drives into one purpose, namely, affectionate union with people and with God and with nature itself. The Sermon on the Mount is a commentary on how to love God and people. "You have heard" the Law, but now it's time to grasp its purpose and meaning. That's what Teresa of Avila did for the Carmelites. That's what we can do for our own families, parishes and workplaces; for the end of the Law is Love.

Prayer

Father of love and law, help us to understand the meaning and purpose of the commandments. Bring us to realize how they help us avoid harming persons and acquire the right inner attitudes. Draw our attention to the love-reasons for law, inasmuch as love is the final goal of all divine law. Show us how the law helps us to stay in love with you and with others. Amen.

Seventh Sunday
of Ordinary Time

Leviticus 19: 1-2, 17-18
Don't hate your brother. Love one another.

1 Corinthians 3: 16-23
The Christ in the "other" makes that person loveable.

Matthew 5: 38-48
Yes, turn the other cheek.

Use the Process of Love
for the Content of Hate

"Love your enemies. It will drive them crazy."

When St. Paul began his career he hated Christ and Christians. Paul was an enemy of Christ. But Jesus always loved Paul, his wildly angry enemy. In the Sermon on the Mount, Jesus preached that one should love one's enemies. On the Road to Damascus, Jesus loved his enemy, Paul, and changed him into a friend.

Why is it important to love an enemy? For one thing, hate multiplies violence and hatred. Love stops the hating. Preach hate and violence to ten men in a row and tell the first man to hit the second and so on. But suppose the fifth man refuses. "He turns the other cheek." He will not pass on the violence or sustain the hatred. He absorbs the wound for the purpose of healing the wounder and stopping the hatred. Jesus gathered up the hatred of his enemies on the Cross and let it strike him in order to save those who wounded him. Jesus teaches that love is a moral power superior to that of hatred.

Christ suggests we look closely at our enemies, for in them we discover our faults. Shakespeare suggests that enemies are our outward consciences. Love your enemy for he or she has much to teach you about yourself. There is more than humor in Oscar Wilde's statement, "A man cannot be too careful in his choice of enemies." Think of the wisdom in the saying, "I can save myself from my enemies, but only God can defend me from my friends."

Jesus wants us to love our enemies not just because they are walking psycho-charts reminding us of our own ridiculousness. Jesus is thinking far more of the matter of reconciliation. He calls us to the highest form of love. Other forms of love, such as self-love, or contract love (I'll do something for you, if you do something for me.) are important, but they do not match the creative love in question here.

Creative love produces love where it did not exist before. Jesus says we must break the cycle of revenge. Instead of trading a killing for a killing, we trade love for hate.

Respond to the content of hatred with the process of love. When attacked with scorn and insult, do not reply with louder curses. Pay less attention to the content of what is said and more to the person saying it. Urge the person to air his or her anger and accept it. Then call for a mutual discussion of what is wrong with the relationship. Deal with the hostile feelings of the other in a patient and understanding manner.

Forget the content of hatred and focus on the passion behind it. Suppress the desire to argue and permit yourself the loving disposition that accepts the person as you find him or her. Shouting matches, often leading to worse violence, are no solution to human relations. Trying to be sensible and logical will not work when the issue is one of intense dislike for whatever reason.

Initiate the process of loving to reply to the content of injustice. So you have been treated unjustly? Will roaring in pain make a difference? Possibly. But most likely the best response is to draw out the unjust aggressor and find out what is causing the wretched behavior. Striking back might make your ego feel better, but it has little to do with solving the relationship problem. Threats and curses have been ruining relationships ever since Cain and Abel. Harboring resentment, bitterness and self-pity changes no one and makes oneself even worse off.

It is not easy of course. But Jesus didn't promise us a rose garden here. (Hereafter, yes.) We must spend most of our life using the process of love to answer the content of hate. That's what loving an enemy is all about. Sometimes the miracle happens. Our love changes the enemy into a friend. What could make life more worthwhile?

Prayer

Lord Jesus, you summon us to the most difficult task of loving our enemies. You remind us by your example on the Cross how your love absorbed the hatred of your enemies and turned that experience into one of forgiveness and hope for all engrossed by attack and counterattack. Make us bold, by your grace, in answering the appearance of hatred with the process of love. Amen.

Eighth Sunday of Ordinary Time

Isaiah 49: 14-15
God has a loving mother's concern for us.

1 Corinthians 4: 1-5
Administer Christ's mystery more than money and things.

Matthew 6: 24-34
You can be free of anxiety.

Why Money and Things Make Us Insecure

St. Frances Cabrini liked to say, "Our Lord is my banker. He will not fail to help me find money." She mastered the lesson of today's gospel: The greatest security comes from trust in God. She had every reason to be insecure when she arrived in New York in the 1890's to found an orphanage. She could barely speak English. She had no money. She did have plenty of faith. She was told by the bishop that the promised orphanage plan fell through. Better she take over a school.

She took the school and also had her orphanage within four months. She found she was a successful beggar and a splendid organizer. She and her sisters went everywhere seeking help from butchers, bakers, fruit stands, clothing stores, the homes of the poor and the mansions of the rich. She looked enviably at the 450-acre Jesuit property across the Hudson, thinking it would be a better place for her orphans.

She heard the Jesuits were moving and planned to sell, because there was no water on the property. Somehow she found the money and purchased the estate and moved her orphans to the country. They washed clothes in the river and set up bucket brigades to bring water to the house. And wouldn't you know it, Mother Cabrini found a well on the property.

She did all this within one year of her arrival in New York. Insecure by worldly standards, but absolutely secure in Jesus, she went on to found sixty-seven other hospitals, orphanages and convents in the next thirty-seven years. She understood completely the message of the "Lilies of the Field," and she left us a life story to prove it.

The poor and materially insecure seem to understand Christ's words about not being anxious more than those who are well off. The richer we get the more we fail to appreciate his words. What happens is that the materially secure become spiritually insecure. Who complains most about the depression that comes from anxiety? Invariably the prosperous. Who crowds the offices of the psychologists? Mainly those who have every reason to be secure and are not. Material possessions seem to capture the owners and make them nervous about their possessions.

Francis of Assissi had nothing, yet he seemed the richest man in the world. He gave away his income and felt better. Throwing off the signs of security he found even more security in God. Why do money and things, the source of our material well being and security, produce the opposite effects?

(1) They demand a lot of attention and care and distract us from spiritual and personal development. The more you own the more you must take care of what you have. But the less time you then have to take care of your spiritual needs. Money and property draw your attention away from other values that need awareness and development.

(2) Money and things touch our penchant for avarice. They cry out to be multiplied and drain away our energies in creating more money and things. Soon they cause in us the idea that our self-worth is measured by amounts. They trap us and make us insecure because there is no end to their demands. We cannot serve God and mammon.

(3) Money and things are perishable and so possess the essence of insecurity—impermanence, loss, instability. Hence the more we have a stake in that which is so *lose-able*, the more we are at a loss about our own lives. Well then, can the prudent individual be secure in sensibly managing money and things according to Christ's teaching?

Yes. Jesus is talking about the abuse, not the use of created things. Saints, like Mother Cabrini, show us the ideal of trust in Christ. We have living examples of people freed from the anxiety that plagues many of us. Thus we know we need not be owned by money and things and so be insecure. Christ calls us to be free, there is no reason why we shouldn't be.

Prayer

Holy Spirit, you bring us the wealth of divine
love and care. Prompt us to see that excessive
involvement in money and things will never
bring us the happiness that is seemingly
promised. Teach us the lesson of the "Lilies of
the Field." Amen.

Lent

Pass the Cross to Me

One of the most moving songs in the musical *Shenandoah* is the revival hymn, "Pass the Cross To Me." That is a theme that suits well the season of Lent with its annual focus on the central mystery of salvation in terms of the Cross and Easter. Since 1960 it has been the fashion to dwell mainly on Easter, just as before that there was an exaggerated emphasis on Good Friday. We are perhaps now ready to put the two together as they should be.

The Risen Christ was not ashamed to retain the wounds of his historical Passion. The historical Christ was bold enough to speak of his forthcoming Easter. As the German theologian Moltmann says, we preach a "Crucified God." Nothing dilutes the message of salvation more than to ignore the Cross or to so smother it with roses and "nice thoughts" that its value and meaning vanish. All great saints and missionaries have attributed their effectiveness to their fidelity to the "Word of the Cross." The self-emptying, self-discipline and self-giving that characterize the Cross are absolute prerequisites for Easter.

All the following Lenten themes touch upon the value of the Cross in relation to Easter and salvation. We begin with the story of the Fall of Man and the need to die to the current taboos against temptation and sin so that we may practice the self-discipline that leads to genuine self-fulfillment. We move then to the theme of covenant in terms of the many self-humiliations of God. This kenosis begins in the Old Testament and finishes in the marvelous and mysterious kenosis/self-emptying of Jesus at Calvary. Thus the ingenious self-humblings of God lead to our perception of His concern and care for us.

In the third week the story of the Samaritan woman's death to her public image and masks led to her salvation. Week four, with its story of the cure of the Man Born Blind reminds us of the need of the learned to die to their pretensions and the unschooled to die to any sense of despair. Neither the arrogance of learning nor the crushing weight of a lack of education should justify the loss of a simple childlike faith. The resuscitation of Lazarus asks us to realize that we must die to the belief that death is the end instead of the beginning and fulfillment of another existence.

Palm Sunday dwells on the Passion of Jesus in the light of the Christian martyrs and the Nazi Holocaust of the Jews. The Easter Sunday Homily both completes the Lenten meditation as well as initiates the beginning of the contemplation of the Risen Lord during the Easter season.

Those who have with sincerity and faith asked the Lord: "Pass the Cross to me. I am ready" are living witnesses to all of us of the full message of salvation. Elizabeth Kübler-Ross described such people in these words: "People are like stained glass windows. They sparkle and shine when the sun is out. But when the darkness sets in, their true beauty is revealed only if there is light from within."

We love Easter but we need the shadows of Good Friday to see the full possibilities of the paschal mystery. The most distant object one can see in the bright light of day is the sun, but in the dark night one can see stars which are millions of times farther away. This is something to keep in mind the next time our private world turns black. We shall come to see much more deeply than we imagined possible.

We conclude with this verse from Amazing Grace:

> "Must Jesus bear his Cross alone . . .
> And all the world go free?
> No, there's a Cross for everyone . . .
> And one for you and me."

First Sunday of Lent

Genesis 2: 7-9; 3: 1-7
Temptation in a garden: Sin.

Romans 5: 12-19
Mankind's disobedience . . . Christ's obedience.

Matthew 4: 1-11
Temptation in a desert: Grace.

The New Taboo: Temptation and Sin

Mark Twain once said, "The only thing I have never been able to resist is temptation." Similar to this is the contention that the best way to handle temptation is to give in to it. These light approaches to temptation point to a nervousness about admitting the possibility of sin to which temptation leads. Laugh sin away and then temptation is just an object of humor.

But sin is no laughing matter. The cruelty that causes child abuse, battered wives, raped women, cheated husbands, traitorous friends or contemptuous bosses causes no cheer in the human heart. Who could look at the humiliation and torture of Christ on the Cross and think temptation and sin should be dismissed with a joke? On Good Friday the world denied, betrayed and killed its Best Friend. What God wanted to show was: We have done this to others. He has permitted us to do it to him. All the sins of the world—all the temptations given in to are writ large at Calvary. On that day we rewrote the Golden Rule: Do unto God what you have done to others.

Every age has its taboos, those forbidden topics and acts, those unmentionable subjects. The greatest taboo today is the topic of sin. The fruit is not forbidden. To say that it is a sin to eat it is a forbidden statement. This is the denial stage in morality. Destroy the awareness of sin and there is no need to speak of salvation, for there is nothing to be saved from.

Today's readings reject the modern taboo and speak forthrightly about temptation, sin and the Fall of Man. The first reading tells of temptation in a Garden of Affluence that leads to sin. The third reading describes a temptation in a Desert of Self-Discipline that leads to grace. The second reading provides the meaning: Humanity's disobedience in the self-indulgent garden is reversed by Christ's obedience in the self-emptying desert.

Augustine says that inside of each of us is a Serpent, an Eve and an Adam. The Serpent is our sensual needs. Eve is our driving passions. Adam is our rational control. The senses tempt us. Passion moves us to give in. Sin is completed when the reason consents. The results harm other persons, our own integrity and our fulfillment in God.

Twentieth-century America, for the majority of its citizens, is an affluent Garden of Eden. Sensuality, passion and a weak reason combine to repeat the Fall of Man story. Left unchecked this will destroy our culture and ruin our lives. America needs the discipline of the desert. Christ shows the way. He leaves the noise of affluence to cope with temptation in the raw. No denial of the reality of sin and temptation here.

God opens Himself to the experience of temptation. His vision and determination are cleansed by the fasting and discipline of the desert. He feels the tug of the tempter and stands firm. He doesn't deny temptation. He denies the tempter. He doesn't pretend sin is unreal. He denies the triumph of sin.

Christ, our God, gives us the example of self-discipline in the face of temptation and sin. He also offers us the power and grace to undertake our own self-discipline; example and power to save us. We yearn for nobility of spirit and the exaltation of heroism. Say yes to self-discipline. Say no to the tempter. Then say amen to the gracious example and power of the Lord.

Prayer

Father of boundless light, penetrate the darkness
of our modern minds which refuse to admit the
reality of temptation and sin. Spur us to reject
the fashionable taboos and direct us to note the
timeless truth about sin and its destructiveness.
By the example and power of Jesus' resistance to
temptation in the desert, move us to do the same.
Amen.

Second Sunday of Lent

Genesis 12: 1-4
Covenant Statement: I will bless and save you.

2 Timothy 8: 1-10
Covenant Response: A holy life.

Matthew 17: 1-9
Covenant Sign: A transfigured Christ.

The Self-humiliation of God

Psalm 18, verse 36 says: "You have stooped to make me great." Thus God humbles Himself to bring about human greatness. Like a mere servant, God walks before Israel in the wilderness carrying the pillar of fire like a torch. God leaves the throne of glory and appears in a simple thorn bush to Moses. He descends from heaven to rest on the Ark of the Covenant and inside the limits of a temple.

Throughout the pages of the Old Testament God is seen as meeting people in trouble, the lowly and unimportant, the nobodies of the world. He carries Israel on His back. God weeps over the tragedies of Israel. He goes with His people into Babylonian Exile. If they go to jail, He goes with them. He feels sorrow with the martyrs and grief with the misbegotten. No human humbling is too much for God to share.

How different is this view of God from other worldly perspectives. The Greeks created an apathetic god who did not worry about people. The Deists forged a watchmaker god who wound up the universe like a clock and forgot about it. Chinese philosophers preached of cosmic silence. One hears no god, only common sense law. The gods of mythology subjected people to fate and blinding necessity. People were just puppets in the hand of a chilling puppeteer.

These gods would not engage in self-humbling. They have no passion or empathy or concern for humans. That is why they never had a covenant. Only a God who could humble Himself would enter into a covenant with man.

The covenant texts from today's readings assume the self-humbling of God. God steps down into the sandals of Abraham, experiences the despairing dead end of this man and his family. In so doing He heals the hopelessness of this homeless family and promises them a future based on trust and belief in that possibility. In Jesus this hope is fully realized by the saving Cross. The covenant sign of transfiguration forecasts the ultimate fulfillment of human hope in God.

Some people want to limit God to a Totally Other. But such a God would be too uncanny, too remote, too weird. A real God makes known His ways. God is indeed a mystery, but He is not too proud or distant to let us see something of Himself. "Clouds and thick darkness are about Him." This is His mystery. "His lighnings light the world. The earth sees and adores." He reveals himself. (Cf. Psalm 97: 2-4)

The concern of God, shining through covenant, especially the covenant of the Cross and its continuation in Eucharist, links God to our human predicaments. God does not leave us alone. The Bible says we are not alone and asks us to believe in God's self-humbling and loving concern.

This is seen in the scriptural theme of the anger of God. We hear not only His love, but His wrath. Not just the roses, but the yells and the hurricanes. This is not the evil anger of a petulant tyrant wanting to scare people. It is the good anger that rejects indifference, complacency and the so-called virtue of unshockability. His anger is the underside of love. God's sense of injustice is more intense than ours. The plight of the poor to us is a misdemeanor, to God it is a tragic disaster.

Our God is not ashamed to share in our humiliations. He stoops into them to bring us life and greatness. This is covenant. This is hope. This is the splendor of the self-humiliation of God.

Prayer

Jesus, meek and humble of heart, make our
hearts like unto thine. Speak to us again of all
the self-humblings of God from the time He
served Israel in the desert to your Incarnation,
and finally to your death on the Cross. Convert
us thus from our own self-exaltations to imitate
your self-humblings and so enter into genuine
greatness. Amen.

Third Sunday of Lent

Exodus 17: 3-7
Israel's trials and way of the cross in the desert.

Romans 5: 1-2, 5-8
Christ identified with our powerlessness to save us.

John 4: 5-52
Woman: "I need a savior." Jesus: "I AM."

Woman, Take Off Your Mask

No one likes a phony. Unmasking a hypocrite gives everyone
satisfaction. To a certain extent, everyone has a cover story that
should be stripped away so that the real person may emerge and
grow. Today we hear how Jesus helped the Samaritan woman
remove her mask and achieve the honesty that brought her salvation. There are three acts in the story: accommodation, confrontation, redemption.

Accommodation—In the first act, Jesus attempts to put the woman at ease. She has at least two reasons to be nervous. She, a Samaritan, alone at a well in a remote place, faces a Jew whose religion she dislikes. Secondly, she is alone with a strange man. Jesus spends time alleviating her fears and creating trust. He comes across as a friendly stranger asking for a drink of water. He offers her the first step to salvation. Think of Matthew 10: 42, "And I promise you that whoever gives a cup of cold water to one of these lowly ones because he is a disciple will not want for his reward."

Jesus moved the conversation to the topic of living water. In the parched landscape of Palestine, living or running water was like gold. In a sense the soul of the woman was arid and in need of the refreshing and healing waters of Christ. More reassured, the woman feels free to argue with Christ. He has no rope or bucket. Does he think he is better than Jacob—patron saint of her religion—who built the well by which they sat? Jesus tells her plainly he can do even better than that with water that slakes the deepest human thirst.

Confrontation—She now seemed sufficiently relaxed. But she was missing his point. Jesus confronted her with the story of her five broken marriages. He removed her mask and disclosed the five disappointments in love behind that cool exterior. Never had she felt such embarrassment. The subject was too painful. Rather than stay on so personal a matter, she switched the conversation to a matter of worship. She had been calling him Sir. Now she calls him Prophet, hoping with the compliment to put him off. Jesus defends the purity of Jewish tradition against the heretical Samaritans. He offers both peoples a new and united worship flowing from the Holy Spirit of Truth.

Redemption—The trust has been created. The mask ripped off. The superficial laid aside. She feels accepted and senses forgiveness. "I seek a savior." Once she had expressed her profoundest thirst Christ was there to respond. Once she died to her fears and shed her masks, she was able to welcome unconditioned love and absolute forgiveness. Jesus says to her, "I am." Divinity, full of love and hope, suffuses her. She leaves her jar, not needed for the waters of salvation. The charms she once used to seduce five husbands, she puts to the work of evangelization. She moved from sin, to Prophet, to Messiah.

The Apostles return and find Jesus pondering autumn wheat. The tips were white with gold and ready to harvest. They urge him to eat his lunch. But he is too full of the joy of having healed and saved the woman. And too full of sorrow for those not yet harvested. In this scene he asks them to pray for evangelists. Another time he will tell them that the grain must die that the wheat may grow.

The scene ends with the local villagers coming to see Jesus. They ask him to preach and then say, "We have heard for ourselves. This is really the savior of the world." (John 4: 42) We all have our masks and our fears. By the grace of this story may we lose the masks and shed the fears and drink of the living waters.

Prayer

Holy Spirit of Candor, Honesty and Truth, take off our foolish masks. Remove every trace of hypocrisy and self-deception from our hearts. Make us see that a false self-image helps no one, least of all ourselves. Treat us gently, but firmly, as Jesus did the woman at the well. Hence by our death to our self-deceptions we may come to holiness and hope. Amen.

Fourth Sunday of Lent

1 Samuel 16: 1, 6-7, 10-13
The Spirit of the Lord rushes on David.

Ephesians 5: 8-14
Move from darkness of sin to light of grace.

John 9: 1-41
Blind hearts, not blind eyes cause sin.

Simple Faith and the Perils
of Religious Learning

Physical blindness often serves as an image of mental stubbornness and spiritual sin. One feels compassion for the truly blind. It is frustrating to empathize with closed minds and hearts. Executives face this when they vainly try to change company policy. Church reformers deal with it in trying to implement Vatican II. Blindness in religion causes prophets to be stoned and angels to weep.

Today's story of the Cure of the Man Born Blind illustrates the perennial problem of the tension between simple faith and the perils of religious learning. It would be wrong to draw the conclusion that simple faith is better than religious learning. Aquinas was just as much of a saint as the unlearned Cure of Ars. Both the uneducated as well as the learned can have closed minds and sinful hearts. The story here is not opposing ignorance and learning so much as an education that causes arrogant prejudice against the unschooled. This is a peril that afflicts both secular as well as religious educators.

Jesus cures a well known blind beggar. When asked about it, the beggar declares that Jesus did it and he must be a prophet. The religious intellectuals were put off on two accounts: the existence of a miracle, and the capacity of a nobody to identify a real prophet. The intellectuals see themselves as protectors of formal religion. They reserve for themselves the right to prophesy and anoint the one they think is heir to the mantle of biblical prophets. They feel, after all, that their long years of study have made them professionally competent to recognize God's work in the world. They can hardly believe such insight has come from a man who never read a book.

They do not intimidate the blind man. Unimpressed, he tells them their studies have closed their minds. They are looking right at a miracle and can't see it. They have seen and heard Jesus and cannot perceive his prophetic quality. All their years of combing the scriptures, analyzing words and talking about laws have not given them insight. They, who should be the light, are blind guides. His forthright simplicity drives them into a rage. "You were born in utter sin. And would you teach us?" (John 9: 34) So they excommunicated him.

The beggar shakes the dust from his feet and goes outside to feast his eyes on the world he never saw before. The first person he meets is Jesus. Christ asks him to believe and trust in him as the hope of the world and the source of love. And the man who could pass no theology exams kneels and says simply, "I believe." (John 9: 38)

This story is meant to praise simple faith, whether it be found among the ignorant or the learned, whether in the hovels of the poor or the lecture halls of a university, whether on the streets of Calcutta or the lawns of Oxford. The learned must die to any arrogance induced by their studies. The unschooled must die to any hardness of heart induced by their unfortunate condition. A person can be closed by the pomposity of education or by the despair induced through poverty. There is a vicious circle for the rich as well as the poor. Both need the openness that leads to the light of faith. Both require the death to self that is a precondition to a personal Easter.

Historians say that today's story was a popular feature of Baptismal ceremonies in the early Church. The physical illumination of the man was paralleled by his spiritual enlightening. May he pray for our faith to give us the light to see as he did.

Prayer

Father of eternal wisdom, rescue us from the
perils of despair caused by our human condition.
Save us from the arrogance of "being in the
know." In a way, we have been spiritually blind
from birth. We seek a healing just as much as the
blind beggar of today's story. You began this
healing in the Sacrament of Baptism. Bring it
now to fruition in our lifelong development.
Amen.

Fifth Sunday of Lent

Ezekiel 37: 12-14
I will open your graves and have you rise from them.

Romans 8: 8-11
The Spirit will bring your mortal bodies to life.

John 11: 1-45
Christ raises Lazarus from the dead.

The Silence of Lazarus

The book, *Life After Life,** by Raymond A. Moody, Jr., M.D., recounts stories of people who apparently died and revived to tell the tale. Most of them speak of some kind of luminous experiences. These interviews with those who have had some kind of brink experience are up-to-date versions of the centuries old attempt to penetrate the barrier between this life and the next.

The remarkable thing about the Lazarus story that we hear today is that there is no news from beyond the grave. The biblical account shows no interest in the trip Lazarus took. No one is quoted about asking him about the sights and sounds of his journey into the realm of death. Nor is he. Nor has he left us any voluntary account of the event.

It might be fair to conclude that either the journey into the next life held no interest for the people of the times, or that Lazarus had nothing to tell them anyway. The biblical account seems more interested in the hopes of the living than in the haunts of the dead. The Lazarus story is less about the corridors of death and more about the vision of eternal life. The atmosphere of the morgue yields to the faith insight into resurrection.

---

*Dr. Raymond A Moody, Jr., M.D., *Life after Life*, New York: Bantam Books, Inc., 1975.

The crucial distinction is between resuscitation and resurrection. In resuscitation our mortal body returns to life as is. In resurrection we are reborn with a glorified body that is still our original person but mysteriously transformed by God's power. When St. Paul was asked the question about what our glorified, risen persons would look like, he resorted to the image of a seed and a plant. The seed becomes the glorious plant, but the seed has achieved an extraordinary new existence. There was enough about Christ's Easter body-person that it was eventually recognizable to the Apostles. But there was much that was different about it to the point that the Apostles didn't know him at first.

We should read the Lazarus story for its dual themes of compassion and resurrection. The death of a loved one always causes grief. Jesus knows such sorrow and is not ashamed to cry when he hears the news and sees the grave. Once again God reaches out to share in the total human experience. God mourns. Yet this is not the whole story. If one has a spiritual life now through union with God, this will continue despite death. At death, then, life is changed, not taken away. Union with Christ here means union with him in the resurrection hereafter.

In recent years there has been so much emphasis on the good and fulfilling life here, there is an impression that either there is no afterlife, or else it doesn't mean much. No one who has a spiritual life, a lifelong love affair with God could believe this or bear it. When one excludes Easter and the afterlife from belief then the death knell for all Christian faith has tolled. It ultimately means we are thrown back on our own resources and condemned to catch what we can before the end.

The resuscitation of Lazarus is a sign of the forthcoming resurrection of Christ and a promise of Lazarus' own *resurrection* after his second death. The momentary reprieve is a stunning miracle to teach us that we need not fear that death is the end of everything. Christ does not free us from dying, but from the threat that there is no more. We will have our Good Friday indeed. But there is a great Easter in our future.

Prayer

Risen Jesus, liberate us from the fear and threat
that face us in our own certain physical deaths.
We are encouraged by the Lazarus story as a sign
of life beyond. We know his resuscitation
forecast your genuine resurrection at Easter. We
are grateful for this encouraging miracle as well
as the full realization on Easter morning. Fix our
memories that we may not forget. Fire our faith
that we may always believe. Amen.

Sixth Sunday of Lent/Palm Sunday

Isaiah 50: 4-7
I gave my back to those who beat me.

Philippians 2: 6-11
He accepted death even to the Cross.

Matthew 26: 14-27; 27: 11-54
The Passion and Death of Christ.

Good Friday and the Holocaust

The New York and Philadelphia public school districts have
introduced a study of the Nazi holocaust of the Jews into the
curriculum. To prepare for that, the writers of the study interviewed survivors of the death camps. One of them was a seven-
year-old boy at the time. He had been in eleven camps. His job
was to dispose of the bodies after gassing. The interviewers were
so horrified they could not handle the testimony. He opened

wounds and feelings too deep. They used professional veneers to fend off further involvement. "Thank you, sir. We will proceed with implementation."

A Catholic nun present at the time felt so bad about this that she went up to the man. She expressed regret and compassion and hoped that he would not feel any sense of residual worthlessness. He thanked her and said: "Each Friday evening, I gather with my wife and two daughters. I bless the bread and a cup of wine and pass them around. And then I kiss my wife and two daughters. That is my Shabbat (Sabbath). This is my heaven. To be alive and know the love of my wife and children."

During this week of the Passion of Christ, we may ponder the martyrdom of Jesus. Or we may ponder the complex types of martyrdoms of various Christians. Or we may take time to dwell on the holocaust of the Jews in Nazi Germany—the martyrdom of a people. While one death, whether on Calvary or in the Roman arena or at Auschwitz is enough to touch anyone's conscience, the incomprehensible cruelty of the murders should sober one's conscience for the rest of human history. Yes, this may sober our conscience. We must also come to cope with such a record.

The immense horror of the holocaust and the possibilities of hope and resurrection find new meaning in the testimony of the survivor quoted above. Millions of good and just people died senselessly in Auschwitz and Dachau. Fortunately, some of these good and just people survived to witness the possibility of hope in the face of a despair unimaginable to most of us.

Holy Week offers us the chance to ponder the death of six million suffering servants of the Hebrew Covenant, along with our brethren from the ancient Roman persecutions, plus modern Communist murders with our good and just Lord and Savior Jesus Christ. Resurrection and hope arose spontaneously from each of these brutal events. Take hope therefore not with the old leaven of sin and hate, but with the new Easter leaven of universal brotherhood and a heart uplifted to the very peak of the universe.

Alleluia means "Praise the Lord." No one could sing it if Christ had not done so at the Last Supper on the Way to the Cross. No one would dare if Christians had not sung it on the way to the

Roman arenas. No one would have the heart, if the man of our story had not told us of his holy Shabbat. The paradox of facing death with faith is that it draws from the dark jaws of apparent defeat the most astounding victories of the human spirit.

Over all of us this Holy Week stands the shadow of the Cross with its unrelieved humiliations. Yet that is a shadow already lined with the bright promise of an Easter dawn. At the hour of compline the monks sing, "In the midst of life we are toward death." Yet by the blessed wood of the Cross we have an Ark that bears us to new life. "Hail O Blessed Cross. We adore thee, O Jesus, for by thy Holy Cross thou has redeemed the world."

Prayer

Lord Christ, crucified God, you sang an alleluia psalm at the end of the Last Supper on your way to betrayal and death. It is the only time your singing was recorded. Show us by this your insight into the bright hope that lay beyond the darkness of death. Stir us to bear with equal courage the Cross we must inevitably carry. We bless and adore you, O Redeemer of the world. Amen.

Palm Sunday

Isaiah 50: 4-7
I gave my cheeks to those who would pluck my beard. I accepted the Cross.

Philippians 2: 6-11
Jesus accepted death on the Cross. Then the Father glorified him as Lord.

Matthew 26: 14-27, 66
Match the outward Cross with the inward motivating love.

An Outward Cross with an Inward Love

In the late summer of 1224 Francis of Assisi began forty days of fasting and prayer to prepare for the feast of the Exaltation of the Holy Cross. Just before this he asked Brother Leo to open the Book of Gospels three times and read what he found. Each time Leo came upon a section from the Passion of Christ. Francis chose those passages for his meditations on the heights of Mount Alverno.

One night an angel appeared to him in a dream. Carrying a violin the angel said, "I will play for you as we play before God." The angel played only one note. It was so full of love and harmony that Francis believed his soul would go directly to heaven should he hear another note. "My soul would have left my body with uncontrollable happiness."

At midnight, when the feast of Holy Cross started, he prayed for two favors. "I ask that I may feel the pain of Christ in his Passion. I ask that my heart be filled with the love that moved Jesus to the Cross, in order to save sinners."

Then a fiery angel came from heaven. Wrapped in the midst of the fire was Christ Crucified. The figure of the Crucified rushed upon Francis and touched him like a lightning flash. Francis felt in his heart the glow of God's love. He found on his body the imprint of the five wounds. He felt the agony of Jesus even as he experienced the purest divine love.

At the beginning of our Holy Week St. Francis reminds us to do more than look at the Cross. We must look through the Cross to its meaning. We shall see the outward pain. We must also see the inward love. Pain alone makes no sense. When motivated by love, pain has meaning. No one can be loved without pain and struggle. The reason why many people give up on each other is that they can't stand the trials and disappointments. But real lovers will go through anything to prove their love. The love inside motivates them to go through the pain outside for the sake of the beloved. Identity with Christ's passion teaches us this lesson.

At the end of his autobiography, *The Seven Storey Mountain,* Thomas Merton imagines God telling him about his death, both in the soul and flesh. "When you have been praised a little and loved a little, I will take away your gifts, your praise, your love. You will be nothing but a dead thing, a rejection. Then you will begin to possess the solitude you seek. Your solitude will bear immense fruit in the souls of people you will never see. Do not ask me where it will be or how. A mountain. A hospital. Gethsemane. I ask this of you that you may become the brother of God and the Christ of the burnt men."*

Merton found his purifying solitude in a hermitage at Gethsemane. He became the "Christ of the burnt men" when he died accidentally touching an exposed wire in his room. Francis bore the Cross of poverty. Merton took the Cross of solitude. An angel of fire branded Francis' body with the Cross. Electrical fire consumed the body of Merton. Both men had their outward Cross and both were touched by the purifying Love coming straight from God. Francis took the Cross to heal us of our possessiveness. Merton shouldered the Cross to cure us of our war-likeness and indifference to injustices. Both men so acted as sworn brothers to Christ.

Holy Week conjures for each of us a vision of Christ and the special Cross he asks us to bear. The Cross stands between the Hosanna's of Palm Sunday and the Alleluias of Easter and in front of the curses of a mob on Good Friday.

Do we find it impossible to keep on loving when it's hard? Jesus did not. Do we have trouble looking for God? Notice that God takes a lot of trouble to look for us. True love asks a big price and gives a rich reward to those who pay it. In the midst of pain listen for the note the angel played for Francis. That is the harmony of God's love that motivates heroic and brave behavior. That is why we sing Hosannas today and will chant Alleluias next week.

---

*From *The Seven Storey Mountain* by Thomas Merton. Copyright © 1978 by Harcourt Brace Jovanovich, New York.

Prayer

Lord Jesus, riding on the donkey of peace into Jerusalem amid Hosannas, you march to the Cross of pain motivated by reasons of love. We mean so much to you that you will go to all this trouble to save us from ourselves. Inspire us to take the outward Cross with the power of your inward love. Move us to love without ever counting the cost. Amen.

Easter/Pentecost

Easter Sunday

Acts 10: 37-43
He ate and drank with us after he rose from the dead.

Colossians 3: 1-4
You, too, are raised up with Christ.

Luke 24: 13-35
They recognized the Risen Christ at Eucharist.

Easter in Sacrament Robes

Recently some have tried to explain Easter in rational and common sense terms. All they have succeeded in doing is to explain Easter away. One should approach Easter with a faith enveloped in love. It is the "beloved disciple" John who is quick to sense the reality of Resurrection. We deal here with the mysterious link between love and knowledge. Augustine proclaims, "Give me a lover and he will understand." The German poet Goethe insisted, "We learn to know only what we love. The depth and fullness of our knowledge are proportionate to the strength, vigor and liveliness of our love." Love is blind only to the obstacles of love. Love has the sight of a hawk when the truth is to be seen.

What are some of the things love sees at Easter? Love sees that Jesus is frequently seen in sacramental or liturgical events. The Emmaus disciples perceive Jesus in the Breaking of the Bread. So too, we see our Easter Lord at Eucharist. Similar to this is the number of times Jesus appears to the disciples when they gather for shared prayer or meals. He shows himself to those who have gathered together in his name for prayer. (Luke 24: 33f) He discloses himself to the apostles as they gather at the lakeside for a breakfast meal.

In John's gospel we see a strong connection between the Easter appearances and the forgiveness of sins—the first intimations of the Sacrament of Reconciliation. On Easter night Jesus appears to the disciples. He breathes upon them the Spirit of peace and imparts to them the ministry of reconciliation. "If you forgive men's sins they are forgiven them. If you hold them bound, they are held bound." Something more than a mere physical movement is meant when Mary Magdalene "turns around" to see the Risen Lord. Her conversion of heart—turning around—is now complete, and so she perceives her Lord.

And who can forget the splendid Easter scene by the lake when Peter who had sinned by denying his Lord three times, now makes a triple confession of love and faith. Thus from John's accounts we can conclude: "Where you experience the forgiveness of sins, there you can know the Risen Jesus to be present."

Hence Jesus is seen in the Sacraments of Eucharist and Penance. He also is seen in the scriptural word. As Jesus explains the Bible to the disciples on the road to Emmaus, they testified that their hearts burned with a sense of the divine presence. Divine power through revelation makes Christ known. The women see an empty tomb. It is the revelation of two angels that tells them the meaning. It is on a mountain, a biblical symbol of revelation, that Jesus commissions the apostles to evangelize the world.

The first disciples were privileged to witness the visible Risen Lord. But John the Evangelist teaches that whenever anyone confesses in faith that Jesus is the Christ and Lord, then that person will meet the Easter Christ invisibly. That is why the last words of Jesus in John's Gospel state: "Blessed are those who have not seen, and yet have believed." Our loving faith gives us the eyes to see the living Christ at Eucharist, Penance, during Scripture reading and in prayer for and charity to others. We also anticipate our own personal resurrection.

Prayer

Risen Christ, you appeared to your disciples in many ways, especially at times of Eucharist, Reconciliation, Bible reading, shared prayer and holy meals. With the aid of angels, the Spirit's power and other forms of revelation's help, the disciples saw you visibly. With the help of that same grace of revelation, aid us to confess you as Christ and Lord, so that we may perceive you invisibly with the loving eyes of faith. Alleluia. Amen.

Second Sunday of Easter

Acts 2: 42-47
The Holy Spirit produces a Community of Faith.

1 Peter 1: 3-9
Distress and suffering mature and strengthen faith.

John 20: 19-31
The doubting Thomas comes to faith.

Faith People Are Alive and Well

On the afternoon of October 12, 1972, a plane carrying a Uruguayan rugby team crashed into the snow of the Andes mountains. Twenty-eight men survived the crash. They faced the terror of sub zero weather. A radio report told them that search parties quit looking for them after eight days. A sudden avalanche killed twelve more of them. The remaining sixteen formed themselves into an orderly society, working together and praying. They said the rosary, convinced that the Mother of God would best understand their need to be with their families.

None of them had been especially religious before. Now they felt a divine presence during their nightly prayer sessions. The severe weather broke after two months. The group elected two strong boys to descend the dreadful mountain for help. One of them repeated the feeling in Tevye's line from the musical "Fiddler on the Roof." "You can make it tough, God. But don't make it impossible." Nine days later, they made it through. By the running waters of a welcome river they prayed aloud to God with all the fervor of their youthful hearts. Within hours, helicopters ferried out the other fourteen boys. They were alive.

This story of religious faith and human courage reveals the remarkable potential of faith. No one could believe they were still alive. Everyone said it was incredible and unbelievable that they survived. Unbelievable—that is, unable to be believed. But these boys believed and lived.

Today's readings center on faith. Acts tells us that the Holy Spirit created a community of lively believers. Peter teaches that distress and suffering will mature and strengthen faith. The Gospel announces that the doubting Thomas became a believer.

A Beatles' tune from some years back has a line that goes, "Look at all the lonely people." That would not apply to the joyous believers of the early Church. It does fit so many thousands today who are robbed of religious faith, and therefore the warmth of community that flows from it. Headlines yell about credibility gaps. In so doing they render a secular verdict on the failure of religious people to offer society a living faith.

Thousands avoid the challenge of a living faith because they instinctively know the personal cost that goes with believing. Peter says, "You may for a time have to suffer the distress of many trials. But this is so that your faith, which is more precious than the passing splendor of fire tried gold, may by its genuineness lead to glory." Legions of people know this in their hearts. Faith is not their problem as much as the implicit, painful challenge that goes with it.

They refuse the risk and the gamble of faith. They cover up their spiritual timidity with the fashionable cloak of doubt. We not only live in a time of doubting Thomases, we seem to glory in it. Christians in the Middle Ages gloried in being the Age of Faith. Today's moderns take pride in being in the Age of Doubt. Why? Because doubt seems so reasonable and sane. Why rush in where it is imagined angels fear to tread? Doubters tend to lack both courage and conviction. Believers forge ahead against all odds. They find joyous community with people and with God. One rugby survivor wrote, "I can assure you that God is here. I felt above all the hand of God. And allowed myself to be guided by it."* He is worth listening to, isn't he?

Prayer

Almighty Lord, rock of our faith and fortress of
our confidence, infuse our wills with your
blessed assurance. When doubt plagues us, reveal
your inner presence to us as you once disclosed
your outer presence to St. Thomas. Confirm our
conviction that you alone are the only One in
whom we can trust without any possible fear of
being let down. We praise you for your love.
Amen.

---

*From *Alive* by Piers D. Read. Copyright © 1975 Avon Books: New York.

Third Sunday of Easter

Acts 2: 14, 22-28
God freed Christ from death's bitter pangs.

1 Peter 1: 17-21
Good freed you from futility by Christ's Passion.

Luke 24: 13-35
Should not the Messiah suffer to enter glory?

The Present Cross—the Future Easter

Back in 1924, the Olympics committee chose an Arlington, Virginia canoe club to compete in the Paris games. One of the members, Bill Havens, longed to go. But his wife would be having her baby while he was away. No jumbo jet could fly him back to her bedside in those days. Bill hesitated. His wife implored him to go, but he stayed with her. The canoe team went without him and won their event a week before little Frank was born.

Bill buried his disappointment in his heart and never spoke of it again. Years passed. Then, in July 1952, a cable from the Helsinki Olympics landed on his desk. It read, "Congratulations, dad. I won. I'm bringing home the medal you lost while waiting for me to be born." Little Frank, born in 1924, had won the main event in singles canoeing in 1952.

Events of sacrificial love never cease to stretch potential of the human heart. Easter follows upon the Cross as inevitably as dawn follows the dusk. No fine young man or lovely young girl ever appears without the hidden stories of countless deeds of sacrificial love making possible their flowering. Jesus says that the grain of wheat must die that the sheaf of wheat can appear. Irving Stone wrote that Michelangelo reached ecstasy in his art only because he committed himself to the agony of creation. Emerson says that nothing great was ever achieved without enthusiasm.

He neglected to add the component of selfless love that is essential to such achievement.

Today's readings dwell on the supreme model of present cross and future Easter. Peter preaches that God freed Christ from death's bitter pangs. Peter writes that God frees us from our futility and aimlessness through Christ's passion. The Emmaus disciples hear Jesus question them plainly, "Should not the Messiah suffer in order to enter glory?" The Emmaus story itself illustrates such a transition. Depressed and agonized disciples come to know the ecstasy of God in the sacramental breaking of the bread.

The message of creative pain and productive Cross bearing finds all too little sympathy in a culture committed to the easy life. Labor saving devices make housecleaning a snap compared to the drudgery of former days. Cars and planes remove the discomfort of traveling. Central heating and air conditioning banish the dread of cold and heat prostrating humidity. The light new fabrics sit easily on the body. TV wraps up the world's information and entertainment for simple digestible consumption, and so on.

All these wonders have a rightful and grateful place in our lives. But they do not banish the Cross. They merely exile it to the fringe of our awareness. But tragedy, pain, despair, anxiety, loneliness and countless other forms of pain come back to haunt everyone. Technology frees people from unnecessary drudgery. It does not solve the fundamental problem of living. The easy life it provides does not prepare people for the sorrows that are to come.

Only daily training in sacrificial love can do that. Instinctively everyone longs for their future Easter. It can only be reached through the present cross. Affluence removes many of the physical hard knocks, but not the psychological and spiritual ones. Only Cross bearing with Christ's grace can do that. Bill Havens waited twenty-eight years for his Easter. It was well worth waiting for!

Prayer

Lord Jesus, by your cross you have saved us from
our sins and foolishness. Hold before us the
example of your commitment to overcome evil
by your redemptive suffering. Firm up our
resolve by your grace so that we may see beyond
the present cross to the future Easter. Alleluia.
Amen.

Fourth Sunday of Easter

Acts 2: 14, 36-41
Peter welcomes sinners and strangers into Christ's home.

1 Peter 2: 22-25
Jesus did not counter insult with anger or pain with revenge.

John 10: 1-10
Jesus the Sheepgate is our Welcome Door.

Christ's "Sheepgate" Is a Welcome Door

Russian writer, Leo Tolstoy, tells the story of an old shoe re-
pairman who made the door of his shop a "Welcome Door." He
had a small room in the basement, the one window of which
looked out on the street. Martin was the man's name. He lived
alone, his wife and children having died. He consoled himself
by reading the Gospels each evening. One night he read of how
Christ was badly treated in the house of Simon the Pharisee. A
woman of the street came and gave Jesus the welcome Simon
had ignored. Martin thought, "If Jesus ever came to my house,

I would make him welcome." Then he heard a voice, "Martin, I am coming to your home tomorrow." Martin glowed with joy.

Snow covered the pavement the next morning. A retired soldier, a neighbor, came and cleared Martin's pavement. Martin invited him in for hot tea and told him excitedly that Jesus would visit him today. They then talked about God. When the soldier left he said, "You have given me food for body and soul!"

Martin peered out his window expectantly. He saw a young mother hugging her baby and shivering against the cold. He invited them in and gave them a bowl of warm soup. She told him her husband abandoned her and she was trying to get back to her mother's home. Martin gave her his wife's cloak and some money for the trip. She said, "Surely Christ must have sent me to your window." Martin watched mother and child go off into the cold.

The day was ending. Martin worried, "Christ has not come yet." Longingly, he stared out the window. An old woman, an apple seller, stood there. Suddenly a boy came to steal one of her apples. She grabbed his collar and yelled, "Police!" Martin rushed out and brought the both of them into his shop. "Ma'm, this is not God's way. If he should be punished for stealing an apple, what should God do to us for our sins."

He told her the story of how the Lord forgave his servant a large debt, and how the servant went out and seized his debtor by the throat, "Don't worry. I'll pay for the apple." The old woman reflected. She thought about how much she loved her own grandchildren. Then her affection spilled over onto the boy. "He's only a child, God help him." Martin watched the two of them leave, the boy carrying the basket for the old woman.

But alas, Jesus had not come. Martin turned on a lamp and took his Gospels to read. A Voice whispered, "Martin, didn't you see me?" "Who are you?" "It is I, Martin." And out of the dark corner stepped the old soldier. "It is I." Martin beheld the smiling mother and the laughing baby. "It is I." The old woman and the boy appeared in friendly embrace.

As they disappeared, Martin looked down at his Gospels where they opened. "I was thirsty, you gave me to drink. I was hungry. You fed me. I was a stranger, you took me in. What you did to the least of my friends, you did to me." Martin realized his dream had come true. The Savior had come to his shop and he welcomed him.

Jesus says in today's Gospel, "I am the Sheepgate. I am the Welcome Door. I turn no one away. I give everyone welcome who comes to me." The application for our own lives is that each of us must be a Sheepgate-Welcome Door to all who approach us. Just as Jesus has received us with an open and generous heart, so must we treat with kindness and understanding all who come to us. The welcome mat in front of the door of our homes is an image of the welcome sign we should wear on our faces.

We should never permit our moodiness or defensiveness to get in the way of making each person we meet feel at home. For everyone who comes to us is Christ in disguise. Just as he shares all the goods of creation with us, we in turn must share what we have with the Christ who comes to us in the shape of others.

The shepherd at the Sheepgate welcomes the tired and hungry sheep at night. Open your heart to welcome anyone who comes to you. For behind every face is the Christ who asks you for sympathy, understanding and acceptance. Put a sign on your face that says to everyone, "Feel at home with me."

Prayer

Jesus, the Sheepgate, you are the Welcome Door
for every human being on earth. Just as a
shepherd waits each night by the Sheepgate to
welcome all the tired sheep home, so you my
Lord wait every moment for us to come to you.
May we have the grace to imitate your example
and be a welcoming people to all whom we
meet. For in welcoming anyone, we welcome
you. Amen.

Fifth Sunday of Easter

Acts 6:1-7
Serve your neighbor as Deacons do.

I Peter 2:4-9
Offer a spiritual sacrifice of works of service.

John 14:1-12
See Christ—see God. See a needy neighbor—see Christ.

Serve Others and See Christ

Serving others requires caring for them. Take the story of Charles Degges. He was a university trained newspaper writer, but Charles died penniless. He spent all his savings caring for his wife who died of cancer. Blind toward the end of his life, he lost his job, and he died a pauper's death in a small room at the age of seventy-three. A Red Cross worker requested a funeral Mass for Charles. But a contract between his funeral director and the public welfare agency allowed no time for a church service.

The contract did allow for one hour visitation at the funeral home. Some parishioners requested the funeral Mass be celebrated there. Forty-five people, Catholic and Protestant gathered. A florist donated flowers. A seminarian brought a choir. The friends carried Charles Degges to his resting place in Potter's Field. He was practically unknown in his dying moments. But forty-five people of the family of humanity gathered to care and say good-bye. After the burial, a man gave the priest a check to help others like Charles Degges.*

So much is said today about Christian service, but a great deal of it is about curing the larger ills of society. It is as though smaller, hidden acts of service are useless and irrelevant. Change the big picture and everything else will be all right. Heal the injustice of the social order and the smaller injustices will be

---

*Story courtesy of Father Richard Martin, St. Leo's Catholic Church, Fairfax, Virginia.

taken care of too. This may be true to some extent, but there is another point of view that says fervor in curing the big injustices will only come from people who know how to show some care for the people at hand. It is possible to love society and not care for people. Such people love ideas, not persons.

Today's readings dwell on the question of service. The Church people of Acts created the deacons to perform acts of service in their community. Peter tells us to offer acts of spiritual sacrifice to God. Are not good works done out of love such a spiritual offering? Jesus tells Phillip that in seeing him, one sees the Father. Do we not come to see Christ, and therefore the Father, in doing works of service and care for others?

Some people serve others in order to get a personal good feeling. But the secret of serving others is to give them a good feeling. The main thing is to bring some loving care to the abandoned, the ignored, and the unlovable. When we do this on a personal level, we are disposed to broader horizons and bigger social issues. We have cured a neighbor's symptoms. Next we reach out to help cure a cultural cause of that symptom, like a doctor who cures a pain symptom with a muscle relaxant, and then cures the cause with an exercise program.

Serve others and see Christ. Care for persons and behold the Lord. Love your neighbor and sense the divine.

Prayer

Loving Father, lift the blindness from our souls
that stops us from seeing the needs of others.
Change us from being self-indulgent to being
persons who happily reach out to serve the needs
of other people. Tell us that we can see you in
looking at Christ. Remind us that we will see
Christ when we turn to help the neighbor who
needs us. We love you. Amen.

Sixth Sunday of Easter

Acts 8: 5-8, 14-17
Phillip brings great news to Samaria.

1 Peter 3: 15-18
Peter tells the world Christ's Good News.

John 14: 15-21
Jesus says the Good News is: You are loved.

Good News in the Heart Means Good News on the Lips

In the winter of 1977, Oxford University invited Cardinal Suenens to give the university retreat. It was the first time a Catholic had been asked to do so since the Reformation. They housed the Cardinal at Christ Church College, a place started by Cardinal Wolsey and finished by Henry VIII. Every day Suenens worked enthusiastically with student groups. Each evening he spoke to standing room only crowds in the venerable seventeenth century Sheldonian theater, designed by Christopher Wren and paid for by Sheldon, the Archbishop of Canterbury.

Suenens spoke on the topic, "My God and Yours." He told his listeners of how he had been touched by Father, Son and Spirit. He spoke proudly of the Church and celebrated the love and values by which the Church had shaped him. At the conclusion of his final conference, the audience rose to give him a heartwarming standing ovation. Then they broke out into a soaring rendition of the great hymn "Come Thou Spirit Divine." University veterans testified they had never seen an outpouring of faith to compare with that experience, within the living memory of their days there.

When a person is intoxicated with God, he or she will seem like awfully good news. When Suenens went to Oxford he brought Good News and touched people with a sense of God's love and presence. He taught them how to sing, "Come Thou Spirit Divine," and they did so with abandon and openness. When the Deacon Phillip, from today's story in Acts, went to Samaria, he brought happiness and hope to the people. He touched their hearts with belief in God and they gladly responded.

When you are full of God, you are full of love. When you are full of love you can barely stop yourself from sharing your affection with others. St. Thomas Aquinas liked to say, "The good is diffusive of itself." If you received a phone call telling you that you had been awarded $100,000, tax free, by the Carnegie Foundation because of your civic mindedness, would you be calm in telling the news to others? Would you wait a week before sharing the news? Yes you might wait to check out the validity of the gift. But once you knew it was true, how long could you restrain yourself from sharing your good fortune? What could stop that happiness from bursting out of you?

Now suppose you have received the gift of the Holy Spirit, the gift of love, the gift of knowing that you are so important in God's eyes that He would stop at nothing to show you His affection. If you are really in touch with that heartwarming news, would you keep it so tightly to yourself that no one around you would know? Suenens did not. The Deacon Phillip could not. No saint ever did.

When news of the German and Japanese surrenders occurred in World War II, did the radios and newspapers keep the stories under wraps? Did the president say, "I think I'll keep this to myself for a while?" Not at all. Reporters raced to phones and poured the good news out to all the world. Announcers rushed to microphones to be sure we knew all about it. Printing presses hummed with special editions. Who cared about the expense. The war was over. Everyone should know the good news right away.

When there is Good News in the heart, there will be Good News on the lips. Full of an experience of God's presence, we can scarcely keep it to ourselves. We will strive to tell the world about the love of God.

If we are not acting with enthusiasm then it must be because we are not sufficiently in touch with the love of God. God tells us the Good News. Hear it. Accept it. Share it!

Prayer

Lord Jesus, you were the first to bring us the
Great News of how much we are loved by God.
When we feel lonely and unwanted and
unloved, wake us up to realize how much
affection you have for us. Let us hear your words,
"I love you," and then share that with all around
us. Amen.

Seventh Sunday of Easter

Acts 1: 12-14
The First Novena. Pray for the coming of the Spirit.

1 Peter 4: 13-16
God's Spirit comes to those joined to Christ's Cross.

John 17: 1-11
Jesus prays for the Spirit to come on his disciples.

Come Thou Spirit Divine

How would you like to wake up one morning and find your own obituary in the newspaper? That chilling experience happened to Alfred Nobel, due to a newsman's mistake. Think of how jarring that would be. Imagine the shock to the man who considered himself the dynamite king and imperious captain of industry. He winced as he read of how the world saw him. People pictured him as a merchant of death who marketed the dread dynamite, making war more horrible than ever.

He pondered his obituary with horror. Not because of the bizarre and premature announcement of his death. But because mankind judged him to be a lover of war. In fact, his whole soul yearned for universal peace. This shattering experience moved him to devote the rest of his life to alerting the world with his dedication to peace. In his last will and testament he left his considerable fortune to promote his ideals. The result was that the world's most honored prize for peace is awarded in his name.

It took a soul-shaking experience to wake Alfred Nobel up to his true vocation in life. The event caused scales to fall from his eyes. He saw himself as others perceived him. To his credit he changed their false impression by permitting an inner-conversion to occur in his own life. We can't all count on a soul awakener as dramatic as his. But we can release the surge of our inner desires that seek a transformation created by the Holy Spirit.

After the feast of the Ascension, we can join the 120 disciples in the upper room whose prayer roared forth from Jerusalem to the throne of light. We can identify with Mary the Mother of God who led the first Christians in prayer for the coming of the Spirit. God planted a profound yearning of Himself in each of our hearts. In prayer we unlock that yearning as though it were an arrow shot from a bow.

St. Peter writes that identity with the Cross makes our prayer more efficient. "Rejoice, insofar as you share in Christ's sufferings. Happy are you when you are insulted for the sake of Christ, for then God's Spirit in His glory will come to rest on you." No wonder Christ's own prayer for the Spirit's coming took place on the night in which he surrendered to the Cross. His own accents in the upper room that night mingled like an echo with the 120 gathered in his name seven weeks later.

Novenas are currently out of style among many Catholics. Yet every year the Church recalls the first and greatest novena, the nine days in which the original Christians prayed for the Spirit's coming. The liturgy does not bow to fad and fashion. Many may have abandoned the primordial nine day prayer. Not the official Church at liturgical prayer. People prone to fashion may forget. Liturgy is immune to such forgetfulness. Instead it stands as a reminder.

Pentecost lies ahead for us. We hunger for the Spirit and wait for a soul awakener. A distressing news item changed Alfred Nobel. More deeply and more regularly, the coming of the Spirit can change us. He forever dedicated his life to peace after his conversion. We can do this and work to witness all the fruits of the loving Spirit of God. We still have seven days to pray. Come, O come thou Spirit divine.

Prayer

Holy Spirit of inner peace, cleanse our hearts
from the petty attachments that turn us upside
down with distraction. Bring us some inner
peace, so we can share that with those near and
dear to us. Grant us the soul sharing experience
that wakes us up to the deep realities of life and
the peace that surpasses all understanding.
Amen.

Pentecost

Acts 2: 1-11
The Holy Spirit enters human hearts.

1 Corinthians 12: 3-7, 12-13
The One Spirit enlivens many ministries.

John 20: 19-23
Accept the Spirit of peace into your soul.

House the Spirit within You

On Pentecost we celebrate and reaffirm our spiritual lives. We renew our awareness of the presence of God in our hearts. The father of the ancient Christian writer, Origen, loved to bend over a child's cradle and say, "I adore God present in the heart of this little baptized Christian." A French Catholic, unable to receive communion, once asked that a poor man be brought to his room, that he might commune with Christ present in the poor. St. Elizabeth of the Trinity writes, "Heaven is in the deepest recesses of our souls."

The Holy Spirit lives in you. St. Catherine of Siena tells of experiencing a violent temptation. When the storm passed, Christ appeared to her. She said, "Where were you when I needed you?" Jesus replied, "I was in your heart." She replied, "How could you have been within me when I was besieged by such detestable thoughts?" The Lord asked her, "Did the thoughts cause you pleasure or pain?" "Terrible pain," said she. "Then," said Jesus, "You know I was with you. Had I not been there, they would have given you pleasure. It was my presence that made the difference. I defended your heart against temptation. Never have I been closer to you."

The saints tell us that their awareness of the Spirit's power within helped them to resist evil. Because they know they are loved, they refuse to betray that love. Is it not likely that people who lose the sense of divine love within will sin more easily for they seem to lose nothing by doing evil?

Good people know that sin brings pleasure. They prefer the greater joy that comes from union with God. Sinners grab the brief pleasure and reap the aftermath of bitterness. They face the law of diminishing returns in which shorter pleasures are followed by longer sadnesses. Christians first face the pain and then taste the joy. The faithless start with an orgy and end up with a hangover. Christianity reverses the process. Celebrate the fast and then enjoy the feast. Christians admit in advance the tragedies of life and turn them into triumphs. Unbelievers imagine there should be no tragedy and wear an injured look when it happens to them. As Nietzche wrote to his sister, "Never forget, my dear sister, unbelief has its tragedies."

All of our Pentecost readings burst with boundless joy and deep peace. Happy disciples tumble out of the upper room, filled with God and ready to tell the world about Him. In the reading from John, we hear that Jesus breathes the Spirit of deep peace and tranquility into the souls of the apostles. Paul tells us that the lively and joyous ministries of the early Church result from the energies granted by the Spirit. But remember that the triumph of Pentecost came after the tragedy of Calvary. The ecstasy of grace came after the painful victory over sin.

The melancholy that rests heavily on so many people today is due to sin and self-indulgence. Sin pays off with lifelong frustration. The sinner is unable to see the possibility of a Holy Spirit within and thus loses the sense of divine love and acceptance. Paul says our body is a temple of the Holy Spirit. Good people know that this thin curtain of flesh veils an unspeakable glory. Thus, with confidence, they live by love. Hence they experience lifelong joy and peace. Welcome the Holy Spirit today, and know a peace beyond all telling.

Prayer

Hail Holy Spirit, comforter and bearer of the
divine gifts. We know in theory that you are in
our hearts. We need to believe this more deeply
so that we can experience your abiding power
within us. We have a way of forgetting you. But
on this glorious Pentecost we beg you to stamp
our memory with your unforgettable beauty.
Never leave us. Always help us. Praise be to you.
Amen.

Trinity Sunday

Exodus 34: 4-6, 8-9
God acts graciously toward us.

2 Corinthians 13: 11-13
Greet each other with a holy kiss in the name of the Trinity.

John 3: 16-18
A loving God gave us His Son to save us.

Praise Father, Son and Holy Ghost

Behind our serene celebration of the Holy Trinity lies a tumultuous history. Fourth century Christianity flared into a raging argument about the Trinity. Prior to the Reformation, no controversy ripped the Church apart so deeply. At the heart of the dispute lay the question of the One God and the meaning of Jesus. One party, led by a man named Arius, claimed Jesus was only a man. Hence there can be no Trinity. In reaction to this another group thought to save Trinity by avowing that Jesus was only God.

Politicians, emperors, theologians, bishops and street crowds threw themselves into the fray as fervently as if they were fans discussing the merits of a favorite football team. The Church found a sensible champion in a preacher named Athanasius and a stout defender in a Bishop named Ambrose. Athanasius used philosophy to defend the Trinity and the divine-human natures of Christ. Ambrose employed music. Athanasius touched the mind with the wonder of the mystery of three persons in One God. Ambrose appealed to the heart with the songs of praise to the most Holy Trinity.

In the city of Milan, where Ambrose was bishop, the streets rang with his songs in defense of the Trinity. He deliberately dramatized his cathedral services with splendid vestments and glorious hymns. In his opinion, music not only soothed the savage beast, it also corrected false doctrine. In using music for religious propaganda, Ambrose fought Arius on his own ground.

Arius was a first class song writer. He composed popular anti-Trinity ditties for the trade guilds, marching songs for soldiers, and theological sea chanties for the merchant marine. Ambrose, equally skilled in writing verse, countered with his own Trinitarian hymns. In our own times we have seen the power of music to push an idea. The protest songs of the 60s stirred the hearts of many and convinced thousands to join the peace movement. And who can forget the persuasive power of "We Shall Overcome" in the cause of civil rights?

You might think the Trinitarian debate is a dead topic of ages past. Yet even now a group of English scholars have published a book about the so-called "Myth of God Incarnate." Like the Arians of the fourth century, they deny the divinity of Christ—and thus the Trinity. A professor in a relgion department of an American university recently lost his post because he denied Christ's divinity.

At the heart of the denial of Trinity is the rejection of God's love through salvation in Christ. Behind all the fuss is the feeling God does not love us enough to become a man and save us. Pushed to its conclusion, the denial of Trinity means "only humans can save humans." Today's readings affirm otherwise. Exodus tells us that God is infinitely gracious. Corinthians announces that a truly loving kiss reflects the boundless love of a Trinitarian God. John never blinks as he proclaims that God's love is so great that he sent His Son to save us.

Americans hunger today for meaningful relationships. The doctrine of Trinity offers us an imperishable role model for loving relations.

Sing praise therefore to the Trinity, as did the parishioners of Bishop Ambrose. It is said that when the angels sing for God, they sing Bach. But when they sing for themselves, they sing Mozart—and God eavesdrops. Without a doubt, when we sing our Trinitarian praises, God eavesdrops on us as well.

Prayer

Most Holy Trinity, you honor us by the
revelation of a community of perfect love. We
look in vain on earth for the ideal relationship.
But in you we can know the mystery of love ever
finding its truest fulfillment. Now that we know
it, endow us with the grace to practice the
mystery. We sing to you a glory that is fitting to
you as Father, Son and Holy Spirit. Amen.

Corpus Christi

Deuteronomy 8: 2-3, 14-16
God fed the physical hungers of a "third world" Israel.

1 Corinthians 10: 16-17
The Church feeds all the hungers of all believers.

John 6: 51-58
Christ fed the spiritual hungers of a "first world" Israel.

The Legend of Marcelino of the Bread and Wine—A Corpus Christi Person

Spanish monks of the Middle Ages loved to tell the story of
Marcelino Pan y Viño, Marcelino of the Bread and Wine. Left as
an abandoned baby by the door of a monastery, Marcelino (so
named because he arrived on the feast of St. Marcellus) proved
to be a ray of sunshine amid the gray stones and black robes of
the monks. As he grew into a lively little boy he also specialized
in mischief: A goat's tail tied to the Abbey bell, lizards in the
salad, a frog in the cook's bed. Friar cook corrected the boy and

said threateningly, "See that stairway. Never go up there. The Big Man will get you."

So naturally one day Marcelino had to go up the stairs to see who this Big Man was. He found him in that dark attic. He saw the Big Man on a cross. The Big Man had thorns on his head and nails in his hands and pain on his face. At first he was scared, then he said, "You look hungry." That night he stole bread and wine from the kitchen and brought it to the Big Man. A light appeared in the Big Man's right hand, and he reached out and took the food, smiling. After that Marcelino took good care of the Big Man. When it stormed he brought him blankets and comforted him.

One day the Big Man came off the Cross, sat down and took Marcelino in his arms. "What would you like most in all the world?" the Big Man asked. "To see my mother," said the boy. "Then you must go into a deep sleep. Close your eyes, Marcelino." The next day, the monks looked in vain for the little boy. The cook thought, "He might be upstairs." Up they went. Slowly they opened the door. The room was flooded with light. Their beloved boy had gone home to see his mother.

The legend of Marcelino of the Bread and Wine brings home to us the essential meaning of our celebration of Corpus Christi. For the little boy, the bread and wine were his way of saying to Christ, "I love you and I want to take care of you." For us, the Bread and Wine are Christ's way of telling us, "I am very fond of you. I want to take care of you."

Just as the boy asked the Big Man no questions, but set out to serve him, because he needed something, so Christ asks us no questions. He sets out to love and serve us. The only thing the boy really hoped for was that the Big Man would open his hand and accept the bread and wine of love. The main thing Christ wants of us is to have us open our hands and take the love he never ceases to offer us.

Christ has taken good care of us. He is bread for our bodies and wine for our souls. Jesus makes it so possible for us to stay in touch with God and to have a life that is worth living on this earth. All we need to do is open our hands and hearts to his Bread and Wine. In return, however, he calls on us to look around us and our world. The affluent United States is thirsting for the wine of faith and a self-image that is worth loving. Americans need to believe that life is worthwhile after all. The underdeveloped nations hunger for bread to stave off their starvation and hope to have a new way of life. They do not ask, "Is life worth living?" They ask, "Am I able to live at all?"

Our responsibility as Corpus Christi persons is to bring the wine of hope to Americans and the bread of nourishment and confidence to the third world. The first world has a full stomach and empty souls. The third world has a full soul but an empty stomach. To the first world we must bring the good works of faith. To the third world we need to bring the faith that expresses itself in good works.

Our theology of liberation means we shall liberate Americans from aridity of soul and third worlders from pangs of hunger. We must make Americans self-reliant in faith. We must help third worlders to be self-reliant in human progress. This is the bread and wine we take and which in turn we must offer. Just as the Big Man was not too big a problem to scare Marcelino, neither must the big problems of Americans and third worlders scare us. Love all the hungry and feed them.

Prayer

Eucharistic Lord, we gratefully eat your bread
and drink your wine, knowing thereby we are
deeply in touch with your love and care. May we
turn then to others in the world and minister to
their spiritual and physical hungers. Let us be
Corpus Christi persons, ready to feed those in
need according to their special cries to us.
Because you are our bread of life, we believe we
can bring you to all who need you. Amen.

Ordinary Time after Pentecost

Ninth Sunday of Ordinary Time

Deuteronomy 11: 18, 26-28
Build your life on the firm rock of God's law.

Romans 3: 21-25, 28
An even firmer bedrock is a living faith.

Matthew 7: 21-27
A wise person attends to a firm foundation.

Sand Christians and Rock Christians

One of the greatest poems in the English language about the subject of solid character is Rudyard Kipling's "If." With lines such as the following, he outlines elements in the rock hard foundation of character building.

> If you can keep your head when all about you
> are losing theirs, and blaming it on you . . .
> If you can meet with triumph and disaster,
> and treat those two imposters just the same . . .
> If you can see the things you gave your life
> to broken, and stoop and build them up again
> with worn out tools.*

Kipling ends his celebration of the virtues of character by saying that the world will acclaim those who followed his advice with the words, "You will be a man, my son."

---

*"If," copyright 1910 by Rudyard Kipling, from *Rudyard Kipling's Verse: Definitive Edition*. Reprinted by permission of Doubleday & Company, Inc.: New York.

Christian character is ultimately a matter of sanctity. It is more popular today to speak of Christian maturity and wholeness instead of sanctity or holiness. All well and good. What's in a name? If the rose of Christian maturity be the same as the scent of holiness, so be it. In either case the strategy for character building demands eliminating faults, deficiencies and sins as well as the positive expansion of one's native virtues. Get rid of what is worst in us. Bring out the best in us.

Saints often found that fighting their worst weakness led to their greatest virtue. Popular thinking tends to associate the value of moderation with Moses. That may have been the new Moses. The old Moses flared with hot temper and anger. He killed an Egyptian because of a sense of outrage at the injustices against his people. He literally broke the Ten Commandments, smashing the tablets of the Law in fury at the sight of Israelites worshipping the golden calf. Yet he turned his hot tempered weakness into a creative moderation.

We all think of John the Evangelist as the love disciple. Yet he was once the power hungry young man who used his mother to persuade Christ to give him a top position in the kingdom. Love is not just for power. Another time, when the Samaritan villagers rejected Christ, John demanded that the Lord destroy the village with fire from the sky. But love is not vengeance. John seems to have once been capable of great hatred. Yet by self-discipline in cooperation with grace, John acquired a character that glowed with love.

Today's readings support Christian character building. Rock Christians build their character on the faith that opens them to God. With faith they put God's voice, that is, the Law and the Gospel, on their foreheads and wrists—on their foreheads to transform their attitudes, on the wrists that God may be in the blood. Thus they will not be sandy, wishy-washy Christians, but rock hard in their personal character.

They pull up the weeds and plant new seeds. Like Ulysses who put wax in his ear that he might not succumb to the seductions of the party girls called sirens, rock Christians fight their weaknesses. Like Orpheus the musician, who played his harp so sumptuously that he drowned out the music of the sirens, rock Christians take the positive approach in acquiring virtue and gospel value.

A Christian, mature in character, is the real superstar of today. No sandy Christians please. Rock ones only, thank you.

Prayer

Father of all, turn us from the folly of building our spiritual lives on sand. With your help, we desire to construct a personal character that is worthy of being called Christian. Such would be a foundation on rock. Help us to see that sandy Christians will never be persons of character nor committed to gospel values. Plant us firmly on the Christian rock. Amen.

Tenth Sunday of Ordinary Time

Hosea 6: 3-6
First the miracle of love, then the homage of worship.

Romans 4: 18-25
First the miracle of faith, then a worshipping people.

Matthew 9: 9-13
First the miracle of conversion, then a Gospel.

Three Calls and One Message

Of the British jury system, Chesterton wrote, "Whenever our civilization wants a library to be catalogued, or a solar system discovered, or any other trifle of this kind, it uses up its specialists. But when it wishes anything done which is really serious, it collects twelve ordinary men. The same thing was done, if I remember right, by the Founder of Christianity."

Vineyards need laborers. Nets require fishermen. Flocks call for shepherds, and fields demand sowers and reapers. A holy people needs patriarchs, prophets and apostles. God chose the patriarch Abraham to tell us of the miracle of faith. The Lord called Hosea to witness the miracle of love. Jesus summoned Matthew to illustrate the miracle of conversion. All were ordinary men transformed by their courageous response to God.

In picking Matthew, Jesus chose a Benedict Arnold figure. Matthew sold out his own people and collected taxes from them for the Roman invaders. He worked on a percentage basis. The citizens of Capharnaum despised Matthew the publican. To them he was a hateful collaborator, a traitor, a sinner. No patriotism simmered in his blood. He forsook love of country to make money off his own people.

The gospel captures Matthew's stunning conversion in one sentence. "Jesus saw a man named Matthew at his post where the taxes were collected. He said to him, 'Follow me.' Matthew got up and followed him." (Matthew 9: 9) The gospel shows no interest in the dynamics of his conversion. It just happens, that's the miracle.

The sinner became a saint. The account executive changes into a gospel writer. The traitor assumes the role of a patriot. Now he loves the history of his people. His new found interest in his cultural and spiritual roots moves him to cite Israel's history no less than 100 times in his gospel. He marshals his historical references into a luminous argument that states: "What a glory our history reveals. Our people have begotten Jesus, the Son of God and Messiah." His country once had meant nothing to him. Now he pours praise on Israel as the locale of salvation. No man could be prouder of his people.

The miracle of transforming grace abounds in today's readings; three calls and one message of grace-transforming power. The obscure shepherd Abraham, through the marvel of faith, becomes a patriarch. The unknown Hosea, reshaped by the miracle of divine love, assumes the mantle of prophecy. The despised Matthew, by the wonder of conversion, receives the gift of apostleship.

Hosea and Matthew discuss the question, "Isn't worship as important as love?" Their answer is, "No. Love has the primacy. Lovers will indeed worship the beloved. Love comes first and all else follows." We live in a time when sloppy thinking habits forbid people to make proper distinctions and put values in hierarchical order. Everything is supposed to be equal. One idea is as good as another. But thoughtful people know there are priorities. Such is the resolution about love and worship. Love will never exclude worship, but mechanical worshipping could exclude love. It was love that transformed the three characters of today's drama. That love will reshape us too. It will make us believers, lovers and patriots. Thanks be to God for His grace.

Prayer

Holy Spirit of vocations and divine calls, speak
to our hearts the vocational challenges you sent
to patriarchs, prophets and apostles. At the same
time, open our resolves to listen and act on the
call you put forth to us. We know that love, faith
and conversion are all works of grace. As miracle
and mystery those experiences are due to your
influence. May we know this glory and live by
the goal it implies. Amen.

Eleventh Sunday
of Ordinary Time

Exodus 19: 2-6
Sinai Covenant. God makes a promise he will keep.

Romans 5: 6-11
Calvary Covenant. Christ fulfills the promise.

Matthew 9: 36; 10: 8
Christ calls twelve messengers to announce a covenant.

The Unbroken Covenant

We live in a time of broken covenants. The high divorce rate records the dreary list of broken promises. Second and third careers imply broken covenants in many cases. Being an "ex-something or other" appears to be a cultural badge. But covenant promises presuppose persistent, enduring devotion.

Take the case of the Scottish blue-collar worker, David Hogg. A century ago, he taught religion class to small, young boys week after week and year after year in the village of Blawtyre. He performed his task with a devotion that was impressive to all who knew him. Out of one of those classes came David Livingstone. He traveled as a Christian missionary to Africa where he marched through the jungles, preaching Christ from village to village. Years later, another missionary came to these same villages where Livingstone had been. As he talked about the life and mission of Jesus, an old lady interrupted him and said, "That man has been here."

The covenant devotion of a village religion teacher in Scotland bred the covenant devotion of a great missionary to the villages of Africa. This was an enduring commitment and a promise kept. That is the key. These were men of character. Contrast this to the remark of a young man to his future father-in-law on the eve of marrying the man's daughter: "I make 400 bucks a week. What do you care whether or not I have character." That father did care and shivered with helpless apprehension at the thought of his daughter marrying so crass a young man. God cares too. In our Exodus reading, we hear God making a covenant promise. One that he will keep. Romans tells us that covenant promise was kept in the Calvary covenant experience. Matthew reminds us that apostles will be needed to witness and proclaim the divine promise that was kept and the human commitments that should be kept as well.

Gandhi wrote, "I hold that a man who deliberately and intelligently makes a pledge and then breaks it, forfeits his manhood. Just as a copper coin treated with mercury becomes valueless when found out, so also the man who lightly pledges his word and then breaks it. We punish the one who diluted the copper coin. The untrustworthy man becomes a person of straw and fits himself for punishment here and hereafter."*

The usual objection at this point is that permanence is an old fashioned value that has no place in a world dedicated to change. Temporary commitment is supposed to be the only possible form of relationship nowadays. There is no room in our brave new world for the trusted pledge and loving promise, or so some of the social commentators would have us believe. "A man's word is his bond," worked all right for Puritan New England or nineteenth century Catholic countries. Not for the twentieth century with its frantic movement of people and information. So they claim.

Life is an ever changing river. No one swims in the same river twice. They are right. The river does change. But there can be something about the person that does not. It is the same person in different water: A person who can love forever and keep his or her promises is such a person. God's promise was an unbroken covenant, ours can be too.

---

*Excerpted from *The International Dictionary of Thoughts,* edited by John Bradley, Chicago: Ferguson, 1973, page 759.

Prayer

Lord Jesus, solidly committed to the promises
you made, enter our lives full of broken
covenants. Dispel the false conviction in us that
it is no longer possible to live up to what one has
pledged. The example of your enduring covenant
should inspire us and the grace behind it should
shore up our behavior in the light of the model
you present. Thank you for this. Amen.

Twelfth Sunday
of Ordinary Time

Jeremiah 20: 10-13
Jeremiah refuses to feel threatened by his enemies.

Romans 5: 12-15
The threat of sin and death is overcome by grace.

Matthew 10: 26-33
Don't let men intimidate you.

How to Handle Intimidation

Intimidation and threat reduce some people to fear and others to inspiring action. When Glen Cunningham was seven years old his legs were burned so badly, the doctors considered amputation. They finally decided against it and predicted Glen would barely be able to walk. "Not only will I walk. I will run." Two years later Glen was running.

By the time he reached college, he joined the track team and broke all kinds of records. At the Berlin Olympics, Glen Cunningham broke the record for 1,500 meter race. A year later he set the world record for the indoor mile. The little boy who might never walk became one of the fastest human beings in the world.

God knows we need experts. But sometimes the rough wisdom of a man such as the late Mayor Daley has its merits, too. "What do the experts know?" There will always be the no-sayers and carping critics who maintain that this or that cannot be done. The young Demosthenes possessed a weak voice and stuttered. Observers intimidated him by telling him he had no future in oratory. We have forgotten the names of his critics. We remember and honor one of the world's greatest orators, Demosthenes, who pushed beyond his weaknesses to master the art of public speaking.

When Beethoven grew deaf, his acquaintances shook their heads. "That's the sad end of his career." Ludwig didn't think so. "I will seize facts by the throat," said he. That's the man who went on to compose the ninth symphony. He didn't hear his soaring ode to joy, but he donated the ecstasy to millions of listeners ever since. The blind Milton didn't worry about his affliction. He composed one of his best remembered poems about his blindness.

These stories of triumph over handicaps and the small, venal opinions of others occur in the area of spiritual growth as well. In our first reading, we hear of cruel threats against the life and purposes of Jeremiah. "All those who were my friends are on the watch for any misstep of mine. Denounce! Let us denounce him!" Jeremiah has no intention of permitting the intimidators to frustrate him. He has found a core of inner power in God and will not budge.

The French writer Albert Camus, overwhelmed by the inevitability of death and the presence of evil, wrote, "The only philosophical decision I can make is whether or not to commit suicide." Sin, evil and death reduced him to so despairing a choice. St. Paul writes for us today that sin and evil and death have been overcome by the cross and the resurrection of Christ.

Suicide is not our goal. Living to the full is our hope. Finally, Jesus says quite plainly, "Do not let men intimidate you. Even if they come to kill you, don't be afraid. They can only destroy the body, not the soul. I have overcome."

There is a right and a wrong way to handle intimidation. One of the by-products of the me-generation is a self-help book that claims the best way to face intimidation is to turn the tables and threaten the other person first. Assert yourself and push the other peson aside. Get him or her before he or she gets you. The teaching of Christ is like a spiritual judo. Accept the attack and turn it to golden advantage. Multiplying threats only produces a jungle. Purifying them produces paradise. Sticks and stones may break our bones, but threats will never destroy us when we believe in Christ's power. God takes care of the sparrow. He will surely take care of us.

Prayer

Father of reassuring authority, rescue us from the
fear of doing what you ask. Save us also from the
intimidation of people who would have us think
there is no possible hope in being virtuous, let
alone any value in it. To the no-sayers around us,
we wish to give an affirmative yes to the
demands of faith and love. With your grace it can
be so. Amen.

Thirteenth Sunday
of Ordinary Time

2 Kings 4: 8-11, 14-16
The lady knows a saint when she sees one.

Romans 6: 3-4, 8-11
Baptism is the beginning of our call to be a saint.

Matthew 10: 37-42
Jesus says, "Admire, welcome, and imitate the saints."

Saints for All Seasons

Modern Cartagena shimmers with all the glamorous luxury of a Carribean resort. Four hundred years ago, it shuddered with the gut wrenching yells of a continuous stream of slave ships. Those boats carried over 10,000 Africans a year to its slave markets. One may notice there today a dark, weathered statue of a Jesuit named Peter Claver. Originally, it had been white marble, but has been darkened by the salt air. Popular tradition says that the black people noted this change with knowing glances, saying, "Father Claver must have been black, for a white man would never have loved us so much."

That was their plain way of saying that Claver was a holy man. The primary traits of a saint are love and service. Holy people know how to love and serve, as is indicated by today's first reading in which a rich lady says she knows a saint when she sees one. So convinced is she that Elisha is a holy man, that she wants him close to her. She is even willing to give him a permanent apartment in her home. He may not have always made the best company; saints seldom do. An old rhyme says, "It is one thing to live with the saints in glory. To live with them on earth is another story."

Peter Claver ran into that difficulty with the parishioners of the Church where the Jesuits served in Cartagena. They were not at all happy when he filled the church with his "smelly slaves." Holy men are not always easy to live with. The barons of the slave trade did not like him at all. He taught the slaves they were human beings worthy of being respected and having their needs looked after.

When he baptized them (tens of thousands of them) he taught them about how important they were before God. That is why they must have self-respect, for they should be treated as important by people too. Claver did not fight slavery directly. He fought it indirectly, because he lectured the owners and sellers they were dealing with human beings, saved by Christ and worthy of care and humanity. He broke the myth that slaves were nothing more than animals. If Christ loved them as people, then Christians must do so too.

Jesus says, "He who welcomes a holy man receives a holy man's reward." Jesus is talking of more than a rule of hospitality. He is far more interested in our welcoming the saint's message into our lives than providing a saint with a subsidized condominium. We only get a saint's reward when we live like a saint, or at least try to do so. As the old saying goes, "It is as important to imitate the saints as to admire them."

Today's liturgy celebrates the theme of the holy person, or saint in the religious life of the Church. In the last twenty years there has been too much downplaying of the saints. There were some good reasons for this. First, we placed Christ as the principal mediator and savior of all back in the center of our religion. Secondly, we pulled away from excessive attention to the marvels and possible superstitions that surrounded saints. But in our eagerness to do these good things, we lost the tremendous value of the saints for our personal lives.

Bring back the saints as down-to-earth human beings whose heads and hearts are full of the love of God and affection for people. Look again at the saints as heart-stretching, inspirational figures who make us want to improve our lives. Look up to the saints as heroes who will motivate us to be more than we are. There are saints for all seasons, for both sexes, for marrieds and singles, for adventurers and contemplatives, for young and old and those in mid-life crises.

Just as love is a many splendored thing, so Jesus is a many splendored person appearing to us under the guise of hundreds of attractive saints. Today is St. Iraneus' feast. He once said, "The glory of God is a man fully alive." Iraneus believed in saints being fully human. He is a good place to start today as we resume our love affair with Christ's holy men and women.

Prayer

Jesus, we love you for so captivating so many
hundreds of men and women throughout the
ages and turning them into saints for our
inspiration and our own personal growth. These
heroes and heroines of the Church tell us there is
hope for profound holiness available to all of us.
They are so human we can scarcely avoid liking
them. They are so grace-full we should rush to
be like them. Empower us to think of them and
pray with them more and more in the future.
Amen.

Fourteenth Sunday of Ordinary Time

Zechariah 9: 9-10
Behold your king comes with love.

Romans 8: 9, 11-13
Behold the Spirit of love makes you a new person.

Matthew 11: 25-30
Behold the love of Jesus cheers you up.

Don't Be Afraid to Accept Love

In Morris West's *Devil's Advocate*, Father Meredith is appointed to his last canonization case. Just before his commission he finds out he has terminal cancer. He asks Cardinal Marotta to excuse him from the case because of his illness. The Cardinal says, "Father Meredith, your real sickness is in your soul, not your body. You have never loved a woman, hated a man or pitied a child. You have not loved, nor shown the need for love."*

Father Meredith admitted the truth of the Cardinal's words. He took the case and resolved to let people he would meet affect him. He succeeded. He brought hope to a bored rich woman. He saved a boy from being exploited. He restored a priest's self-respect. And each of them gave him a feeling of being wanted and loved.

He let people walk into his life and found out that he was a better man for it. As Dinah Shore once said, "Trouble is a part of life. If you don't share it, you don't give the person who loves you a chance to love you enough." Meredith let others love him, and the burdens of his heart were lightened.

Jesus begs us today to permit him to walk into our lives. Jesus invites us to share our heavy hearts with him. He promises that he will love away the heaviness and make the burdens we have seem light. Christ's affection for us will turn our fatigue into vitality and our boredom into a fresh interest for living. Why? Because Jesus loves us and that is what true love always accomplishes.

Too many people rush toward love with open arms, but then hide from it when it is offered. Why does this happen? Because we have been betrayed too often. Too many people have let us down. We fail to accept another's love because we cannot trust them. We do not believe they really mean it. So we are paralyzed by fear. We cannot take the chance. The real opposite of love is fear.

---

*West, Morris, *The Devil's Advocate*, New York: Dell Publishing, 1959, page 34.

People normally think that hate is the opposite of love. In a sense it is, but in another sense hate is very close to love. Good haters can make good lovers. But aggressive fearers make terrible lovers. They are too afraid to love. They are too frightened to get involved, and too tender about being hurt.

They hear the beautiful words of Zechariah, "Rejoice, O daughter of Zion. Behold your king comes to you with love and affection. He rides not on the horse of control and betrayal, but on the simple ass of humility and gentleness" (first reading). They hear these words and want to believe, but they hold back. They are afraid.

Another reason why people are scared to accept love is they think they are too weak to return it. They feel they will be smothered. They are convinced they have no power to match love for love. Feeling so helpless about living up to the demands and ideals of love, they refuse to have a love relationship. Unable to give love—or so they think—they will not take love. They have not understood that another's love creates within them the ability to return love. They do not appreciate Paul's advice to the Romans about letting God's Holy Spirit of love into their hearts so they can rise from the death of unlove.

Thus fear and mistrust cause the heavy heart. Those unable to love mistrust the offer of love from another. They also mistrust their own ability to love. They fear others and are frightened about themselves. Fear freezes their hearts. Scared beyond reason, they cannot have the faith that permits them to take the gamble and the risk of love.

Faith is the key to love. Faith is the ability to believe one is loveable and able to love. Faith permits us to take the risk of love. All love comes from God originally. Believe this. Trust in this. Don't be scared. Let Christ walk into your life. Then you will be able to let people affect you and love you. And with their gift of love, you will begin to love them as well.

Prayer

Father of love teach us to realize our need for
love. Help us to be courageous enough to let
others walk into our lives and bring us love and
vitality. Help us to see that we need not be afraid
either of others or ourselves. You have authored
all the love that comes to us through people.
Open our hearts to be treasuries into which love
is poured, so that we may then return gladly the
rich gifts we have received. Amen.

Fifteenth Sunday of Ordinary Time

Isaiah 55: 10-11
God's Word is the seed of Love

Romans 8: 18-23
When our agony is associated with love, a new person is born.

Matthew 13: 1-23
Jesus details our defenses against his love.

Your Defensiveness Will Destroy You

There is a legend about a turtle and a scorpion facing a swollen river. The scorpion begged the turtle to carry him across the river on his back. The turtle refused. "No, I won't take you because you will sting me." "Why would I do that?" said the scorpion. "You would be my life raft. If I stung you we would both drown."

"Well, since you put it that way, I guess it's all right. Jump on."

So the scorpion boarded the turtle's back and they moved across the river. But just before reaching the shore, the scorpion stung the turtle and they both began to sink in the torrent. The turtle said to the scorpion, "Before we drown, I have to know why you did this to me. Why did you do it?" Possibly a little embarrassed, the scorpion said, "I really don't know. What can I say to you? I couldn't help myself. It's my nature."

Inside all of us lies a scorpion, a beast, a stinger. Another word for all of this is defensiveness. We use our stings, our yells and roars to defend ourselves from other people. There may be some value to this at times, especially when we are put upon or unjustly treated. The growl inside us stems from our need for survival. Our protectiveness is part of our nature. The problem is that we use these stings and frowns too often and in the wrong situations. We are too indiscriminate. We use our defenses not just to ward off enemies. We also employ them to keep friends and those who would love us at bay.

We sting our families, spouses, children, friends—and God. They come to us with love. We repel them with psychological napalm. The Bible tells us that the Word of God is a word of love, a whisper of affection. The Bible compares the Word of God to a seed, an image that any farmer or gardener will appreciate.

Jesus says that his love seed, his love word, meets three kinds of defenses: (1) a hardened road, (2) a pile of rocks, (3) a thorny bush. Jesus tries to love us, and we tighten our hearts. Or we throw rocks at him to keep him at a safe distance. Or we sting him with the thorns of our defensiveness. We do the same with others.

All too often we act like wounded animals, suspicious, waiting for the other person to strike. In too many cases we are much too frightened of the people around us—and of God. Perhaps we have lost so many battles, we feel compelled to be armed against anyone who would offer us love. Having lost out so much in our quest for love we are convinced it can never happen to us. We use violence to resist the only force—love—that could save us from being violent.

Thus the seeds of love that are offered to us are eaten up by others—the birds of the air. Or they are scorched by the sun—the burnt feelings of those who would care for us. Or they are choked by thorns—the words of understanding are shoved down the throat of the speaker. We are perfectly capable of doing this both to Christ and to those close to us. The pity of it all is that we are so anxious to sting others, we miss the kindness that could be ours for the asking.

So many of us have turned our lives into an arms race. We use the political model of nuclear deterrent instead of the Gospel model of loving acceptance. We each carry clubs, waiting for the other to lay down his or her club. We forget that in personal relationships just carrying a club is enough to guarantee someone will rap us on the head.

Life does not have to be this way. We have the choice of being *good ground*. We can pull in the sting, lay down the club, suppress the growl and humbly accept the love and understanding that is offered us. We tend to think that is losing a battle. Actually, it is winning a war.

Prayer

Lord Jesus, your word is love. You have
compared your love-word to a seed that meets all
kinds of defensiveness in ourselves. We use our
survival mechanisms, our stings, growls and
clubs to keep you away from us. Show us how to
let down our walls so we can come to experience
the warmth of your divine affection. Then we
will know how to receive the same from those
around us. Amen.

Sixteenth Sunday of Ordinary Time

Wisdom 12: 13, 16-19
The master of might judges with mercy.

Romans 8: 26-28
Ultimately all works for the good of the world.

Matthew 13: 24-43
Don't get too upset about the weeds in the Church wheat.

How to Handle Weeds in the Church's Wheat Field

Some people are so disgusted with the faults, sins and corruption they see in the Church that they resort to extreme solutions. They either leave the Church, or they want to drive out the sinners. They cannot stand weeds among the wheat.

Joan of Arc faced some pretty tough weeds in the Church of her day. Responding to a call from God to help end the Hundred Years War, the curse of the fourteenth century, Joan became the commander of the French forces.

In time she was captured by the English and put on trial as a heretic. Church leaders were fully prepared to destroy her. They intimidated her, but she proved a sturdy witness in the witness stand. They asked her to swear on the Gospels that she would speak nothing but the truth. She said she did not know what they wanted to ask her. "Perhaps you will ask me things that I will not tell you."

An Inquisitor threatened her with the question, "Do you think you are in the state of grace?" The nineteen-year-old Joan replied with the subtlety of a theologian: "If I am not, may God put me there. If I am, may he keep me there." She shot these remarks at the "weeds"—a court composed of one cardinal, six bishops, thirty-two doctors of theology, sixteen bachelors of theology, seven doctors of medicine and one hundred three other accusers.

Frustrated, they reminded her that they were the Church. She gazed at them as though they were a bunch of roosters at sunrise in her farmyard at Domremy. She looked beyond them to the truth of the matter, "To me the Church is where Christ is. There can be no contradiction between Christ and his Church." They burned her at the stake for her impudent remarks.

Twenty-five years later, a Church court reversed this judgment about her presumed heresy. In 1920, she was canonized a saint and made the patroness of France. Joan understood there were weeds with the wheat in the Church. It was not a perfect Church. She was comfortable with that, despite the suffering that it caused her. She made her insight the road to sanctity.

This is the meaning of the parable of the weeds and the wheat. We have a Church that has saints and sinners and everybody in between. Our Church is not an elitist band of angels, nor a wretched company of the damned. We have chaos amid our cosmos. We do try to stamp out sin and evil, but in doing so we must not destroy the Church itself.

The sinners among us can become saints. The saints among us can become holier. No one is in a fixed state this side of paradise. The sinners need our forgiveness and the saints our admiration and resolve to change.

The French have a saying, "To understand everything is to forgive everything." We are called to appreciate the whole picture of the Church that is composed of people on a journey. Some are racing toward God. Others are speeding away from him. Others are muddling through. The drama and adventure of being a Catholic is to walk this journey with poise, elegance, sympathy and understanding.

When we feel the impulse not to forgive, it is time to look into our own hearts and find out why we are being so zealous. It is time to ask ourselves, "Where is our gift of loving forgiveness? Where is the heart that reaches out with empathy to heal our brothers and sisters? Where is our inner resource that blocks unseemly judgmentalism?"

Fanatics are like forest fires. They burn brightly, but destroy all that is tender and green. To be useful, fire must be confined. The passion for goodness must be linked to the compassion for people. That is the best way to handle those weeds we see in the wheat of the Church.

Prayer

Holy Spirit of compassion and understanding,
we need your assistance when faced with the
faults and sins we see in our Church community.
As you once gave Solomon an understanding
heart, so endow us as well with the sympathy we
need to bring the healing touch of forgiveness to
sinners. May we remember that we are sinners
ourselves and thus should be the last to throw
stones. Give us the insight to accept a Church
that will have weeds as well as wheat. Amen.

Seventeenth Sunday of Ordinary Time

1 Kings 3: 5, 7-12
God unlocks the hidden wisdom in Solomon's heart.

Romans 8: 28-30
God brings to awareness the Christ-Image in us.

Matthew 13: 44-52
The greatest treasures are buried deeply in life.

Bring Forth the Hidden Greatness

In thinking about greatness, Mark Twain once advised a friend: "Keep away from people who try to belittle your ambitions. Small people always do that. The really great make you feel, that you, too, can become great." Twain was right. The inner greatness of each person needs the encouragement of other generous hearted people to call forth that inner treasure.

Shakespeare says that "Some are born great. Some achieve greatness. Some have greatness thrust upon them." (*Twelfth Night*, Act II, Sc. 5) He might well have added that some are the lucky beneficiaries of insightful people who notice the talent and urge it forth.

The founder of Temple University was a minister who developed only one major speech in his life. He repeated this one talk all over the United States. The name of the talk was "Acres of Diamonds". He based his presentation upon the story of a man who looked everywhere he could to find success, never realizing there was a diamond mine on his own property. The point of the story: there are acres of diamonds inside every human soul. There is a treasure hidden in the field of every human person. This preacher devoted his life to waking people up to the God given treasures already possessed by each of his listeners.

What is this greatness? What are the talents? How is one to speak of the acres of diamonds today?

The inner greatness is a holy trinity of one's self-worth, one's talents and one's awareness of the kingdom of God within. Millions of Americans walk around believing they have no self-worth. For a number of reasons they feel bad about themselves. They are depressed by a poor self-image. Moreover, thousands of other Americans feel underdeveloped. They sense they have many talents that no one has ever recognized. Lastly, there are all too many American Catholics who somehow have missed the dramatic truth that the kingdom of God is within them. The spiritual desolation that results makes the other disappointments even more acute.

The problem about these values of self-worth, talent, and spiritual kingdom is that each of these treasures is buried in the field of the heart. They are out of sight—and for all too many, out of mind. In order to get the treasure out, there has to be some digging. One needs an oil drill to get at the black gold. One requires a shovel to dig into the earth.

One cannot use physical tools to unearth the spiritual values under consideration. One must employ spiritual tools. And it helps so much if others come to the rescue. This is where loving and believing and interested people come into the picture. One of the old songs says, "Speak your love to those who seek your love." Bring forth the hidden greatness of others. Realize that, "You're nobody till somebody loves you."

The combination of faith and loving care calls forth the pearl of great price that is our God-given self-worth. It summons to light the buried treasure of our discovery that the kingdom of God is within us. God unlocked the hidden wisdom in Solomon's heart to make him the world's wisest king. With God's help you can unearth the acres of diamonds in your neighbor's heart. What a gift you have. Pray, use it!

Prayer

Lord Jesus you have taught us that the greatest
wonders are usually hidden deep within the
person, like a treasure buried in a field. Because
the beauty is so far out of sight, it tends to be out
of mind. May we follow your grace-filled advice
and call forth the hidden treasures of greatness
and divine kingdom planted inside persons to
bring them the fulfillment they so earnestly
merit. Amen.

Feast of the Transfiguration

Daniel 7: 9-10, 13-14
A vision of the Son of Man clothed with the sky.

2 Peter 1: 16-19
Peter's memory of the transfiguration.

Matthew 17: 1-9
Transfiguration of Jesus.

Beauty Comes from the Inside

Some people seem to have an aura about them. This can come from imposing physical presence as in the case of a pro football player. Or it may arise from the dazzling beauty of a movie star. Again it may proceed from the inner radiance of a very good person. Such people seem to fill a room when they walk into it. It is common enough for others to hold their breath a moment and then say, "I felt a light surrounding that person."

By adverting to such examples from our everyday experiences, we can gain some insight into the exceptional experience of Peter, James and John on Mount Tabor. If any person of history could be expected to have an aura about him, it would most certainly be Jesus. On the summit of Mount Tabor, Jesus needed no spotlight to draw attention to his presence. His divine radiance burst forth from within.

A church has been built in the Holy Land at Mount Tabor to memorialize this sacred event. The architect commissioned experts in mosaic work to do a representation of the transfiguration scene. The artists chose chips that would collect and reflect light. Hence when the morning sunshine streams through the clear windows of the Church and touches the mosaic, the garments of Jesus again seem to glow like snow, and his face to shine as the sun.

All the gospel stories note that Moses and Elijah appear with Jesus and talk with him. When Moses had spoken with God at Sinai, the divine radiance clung to his face so brightly that he needed to veil it until the light passed. Elijah had journeyed to heaven in a chariot all alight with the divine fire. St. Luke notes that these two men spoke with Jesus about the destiny he would fulfill in Jerusalem.

That destiny was, of course, the salvation event of the passion, death, and resurrection. Most Fathers of the Church teach that Jesus permitted these three apostles to see his inner glory to help them cope with the forthcoming trauma of the Passion. It is those same three who will be with Jesus when he agonizes one last time over the decision to take the "cup of sorrow" at Gethsemane.

No agony, however, at Tabor. The mood is joy. Jesus seems glad to be making this decision. It is like the joy that took hold of the patriarch Jacob when he saw his son Joseph, moving him to say, "Now let me die." It is very similar to the peace that flooded Simeon when he held the child Jesus in his arms and recited the words, "Now let my soul depart in peace." We are reminded of the soldier, Agamemnon, in the Greek play who returned home from the Trojan war—and in his joy claimed he was willing to die.

Shakespeare put similar words on the lips of Othello after the perils of a voyage:

> *If it were now to die . . . 'Twere now to be most happy;*
> *for, I fear*
> *My soul hath her content so absolute*
> *That no other comfort like to this*
> *Succeeds in unknown fate.*

Like the three apostles we are reminded that ultimate inner radiance is bought at the price of an encounter with sorrow, pain—even death. The crown comes after the Cross. Peter's words in the second reading state the meaning well: "Keep your attention closely fixed on it, as you would a lamp shining in a dark place . . . until the first streaks of dawn appear, and the morning star rises in your hearts."

Prayer

Holy Spirit of love, we have been taught that our body-persons are temples of your presence. All too often we stand on Tabor, but never let the glory of your presence shine through. Teach us to go through our personal cross which is the key that unlocks inner beauty. Amen.

Eighteenth Sunday of Ordinary Time

Isaiah 55: 1-3
Come without paying and cost. Drink wine and milk.

Romans 8: 35, 37-39
Nothing need separate us from the love Christ has for us.

Matthew 14: 13-21
Come, be the guest of Christ at his family meal.

Examine the Quality of Your Family Meals

To give someone food is to give them love. Bread sharing is person sharing. Dorothy Day became famous for her attempts to reform the social order. At the same time she was always performing her own "miracle of the loaves and fishes." She always managed to find food for the poor who thronged to her soup kitchen at Maryhouse on New York's Lower East Side.

Dorothy Day and her workers always lived and ate alongside their "guests." When her shoestring operation ran out of funds, she prayed to St. Joseph for help, and donations somehow appeared. Standing in the overflow crowd outside the Nativity Church at her funeral was a drifter named Lazarus. Said he, with tears oozing down his lined cheeks, "That fine lady gave me love."

St. Matthew says that Christ's heart "was moved with pity" when he saw the needs of people. His miracle of the loaves was an act of compassion and love. The feeding of the five thousand was a huge family meal with Christ as presider. Scholars call the event a messianic banquet. In his teachings and parables Jesus would speak of a banquet as an image of the kingdom of heaven, the kingdom of love, justice and mercy.

One of the lessons to be drawn from this event is the importance of the family meal. Just as the table of the Eucharist stands for union with the love of Christ, so the table of your home stands for union with each other in love. To be given a seat at the family table is to experience welcome, love and acceptance. In the 1967 movie, "Guess Who's Coming to Dinner," Spencer Tracy and Katherine Hepburn are faced with the challenge to accept Sidney Poitier as a welcome and accepted guest at their table—and a possible future son-in-law.

The humor, pathos and inspiration of the movie derives from their successful struggle against their racial prejudices. They must learn to make their table a place where a black man can feel welcome and accepted. To do that, they must make a place for him in their hearts. They do, in fact, overcome their narrow prejudice and make their bread sharing a time of person sharing with this new man in the house.

The miracle of the table in most homes today comes when families take time to eat with each other and show each other some love and welcome. So many people today are living on the fast track that they have forgotten the beauty and dignity and wonder of a meal where the family members take time with each other. Newspapers, TV's and meetings break up the family so much that the idea of a family meal seems almost quaint—a memory of the past.

No simpler method of communication and family communion has ever been invented than the family meal. In less frenzied times, the culture favored such a meal. Today families must work on planning the gathering of the members and agreeing to spend time with each other while enjoying the meal. Families tend to do this with great seriousness at Thanksgiving, Christmas and other big occasions. It would be just as wise to make the family meal a more normal event. Father Peyton says that the "Family that prays together stays together." One might also say that the family which dines together will stay together too.

Jesus created a huge family meal on a Galilean hillside to show how much he thought of eating with one another. Then he went on to create the Sacrament of Eucharist at a family meal with his apostles. He shared his power in the bread miracle. He shared his very life in the bread mystery of the Eucharist. In both cases he was showing boundless love. He was also telling us a deep truth about ourselves: Bread sharing is person sharing. Examine your family meal and see what it tells you about your lives as a loving, affectionate and welcoming group.

Prayer

O Bread of life and love, you held a great family
meal for five thousand on a Galilean hillside.
You showed us there that bread sharing is person
sharing. At the Last Supper you created Eucharist
in a setting of a family meal. You taught us that
person sharing requires sacrificial love. Bring
home again to us the meaning of a family meal
with its qualities of love, welcome and
acceptance. Amen.

Nineteenth Sunday
of Ordinary Time

1 Kings 19: 9, 11-13
Elijah hears God in a whisper.

Romans 9: 1-5
Paul's concern for his Jewish brethren.

Matthew 14: 22-23
Peter hears Jesus in the storm.

What Wakes Us up to God?

People will try every solution to life's problems before they turn to God. So many answers have been sought in education, the new morality and the powers of reason.

Education has appeared to many to be the road to personal success. Now that schooling is possible for everyone in America, it becomes clear there is a collection of problems no one anticipated. Lots of education, so little truth. We cram children's minds with facts but seem afraid to help them learn how to live. We have dropped discipline because it degenerated into mere punishment. We have forgotten that discipline can be therapy.

We have eliminated morality and values from public education and produced walking encyclopaedias instead. But the walking books have heads full of the straw of facts ready to be inflamed by any demagogue or pitchman that comes along. We enjoy stocking their minds. We dread training their characters.

And then we wonder why 18,000 young people every year die in traffic accidents—twice as many deaths as are caused by all other accidents combined. We fail to note why 4,000 youths a year commit suicide and that nearly half a million others try.

We hear a lot about drugs and teenage alcoholics, yet still do not think that family life or valueless education has anything to do with the problem. Education, of this kind, has not saved our young.

Then comes the new morality to save us. Some of it may have a grain of hope, but a good deal of it is simply changing the standards to fit our new immorality. Frankly, it is impossible to teach morality without the religious faith that gives it motivation and personal courage. That is why the new morality is failing. Without a God to relate to, people are thrown back on themselves and "do their own thing." When humanity becomes the standard of morality instead of God, small wonder the measure is both fickle and unimpressive. The new morality, in this sense, will not save us.

But what about the powers of reason? This might be of some use if people would use their reason to ponder the purpose of life. But practically everyone is using their mind for less noble endeavors. The energies of the human mind today dwell on making money, seeking new thrills, upstaging neighbors, trying the latest fashions and searching for ways to avoid boredom. If reason were used to wrestle with the why's of life, it might help people to live more deeply and with some sense of satisfaction.

So we come back once again to faith in God and trust in Christ. Today's readings tell of a depressed Elijah and a confused Peter. Elijah has finished what should have been a brilliant career as a professional religious person. Everything seems to have gone wrong. He tried to educate the people and somehow education didn't work. God told him, "Wait till you hear my voice and I will bring you peace." Eventually Elijah hears God in an undramatic and quiet whisper. He is called to faith.

Peter, using his reason to solve his impetuosities, thinks he can walk on water. He should have had enough sense to know that in a storm he couldn't even swim. Jesus calls to him through the storm and saves him. He rebukes him for forgetting faith, a perennial truth. Faith is the road to ultimate salvation. "I believe Lord, help my unbelief."

Prayer

Father you will speak to us in many ways.
Sometimes you beat us over the head as you did
Peter in the storm. Other times you come quietly
in a whispered breeze as you did to Elijah on
Mount Carmel. Either way will work if we will
be open to your loving advance. Do not spare us
O Lord. Keep coming and give us the good sense
to listen. Amen.

Feast of the Assumption

Revelation 11: 19; 12: 1-6, 10
A woman crowned with glory.

1 Corinthians 15: 20-26
Paul teaches about resurrection.

Luke 1: 39-56
Mary gives glory to God.

Why Pray to Mary? Why Not?

Almost every child has known the joy of having his or her
mother promise to bake him or her a chocolate cake. The child
may well watch her as she mysteriously combines flour, sugar,
butter, chocolate and other delicious ingredients. The child
moves in close as she whips up the batter. Then his or her mother
says not to touch the batter. Wait for the cake. Don't take what
might make you sick. And just as inevitably, practically every
child will eat some batter, and some may get sick. The batter is
not bad in itself, but the cake is better.

The story of Adam and Eve revolves around much the same truth. None of the fruit in the garden of Eden was bad. But some of it was in an imperfect state like the cake batter. It had not yet reached its final purpose. Adam and Eve engaged in an act that ignored final purpose as have all people, save Jesus and Mary. Thus sin pervades the world. People are at cross purposes with God. Just as a child thinks him or herself wiser than his or her mother, so mankind believes itself wiser than God.

The result is an eviction proceeding in which love is driven from the heart. The first stage is to ignore God and exile His love from our souls. The next moment we ignore people and drive love of them from our awareness. The daily paper reports the public sins of nations and persons: terrorists in Belfast and Tel Aviv, thieves in the government, kidnappings, murders, rapes, child abuse and battered wives. Who would deny that love has been driven from the heart and replaced by sin?

Jesus has redeemed us from slavery to sin. We can and should pray to him for forgiveness and delivery. We can also pray to Mary to help us approach God, should He seem to us too awesome. On this feast of the Assumption we celebrate the final glory of the woman who lived without sin and was the mother who gave birth to and raised a Savior. She sings of her own approachableness in the Gospel: "He has looked upon his servant in her lowliness." Even on the day of her glory, the Church repeats her words about humble nearness to us.

Nathaniel Hawthorne writes, "I have always envied Catholics that sweet, sacred, Virgin Mother, who stands between them and the deity. She intercepts somewhat His awesome splendor. She permits his love stream on the worshipper through the medium of a woman's tenderness." God is, of course, approachable too. But for those who have not yet the insight to see it, the Blessed Mother will help.

George Bernard Shaw was a great friend of a mother superior of a convent. He confided in her that he found it so hard to believe in the divinity of Jesus. But then he said, "I think his mother will see me through." For those who are not quite ready to approach Christ, they can find solace in conversing with the Mother of God. The novelist Marcel Proust recalled that he would tell his mother about the many evils he performed in ignorance and passion. She always seemed to listen with a forgiving under-standing. Her gentleness lessened their importance and lifted the weight from his conscience.

The same is true with prayer to Mary, the spiritual mother of Christians. She listens to us with all the sympathy that any mother would give. She then draws us into the orbit of her Son where we feel the astonishing acceptance and forgiveness of the saved. These periodic feasts of Mary are meant both to honor the events of her life on earth and her glory in heaven. They are also meant to disclose her interest and sympathy for us. Holy Mary, Mother of God . . . Pray for us!

Prayer

Holy Mary, we find it hard sometimes to speak to God. For whatever reason He may seem too absolute, too stern, too much for our frail spirits. We are grateful for your glorious presence in heaven. Despite your exaltation and glorious honors, you still seem very down to earth, just as our human mothers always are. Thank you for staying near us and never cease to draw us to Jesus and the Father. Amen.

Twentieth Sunday of Ordinary Time

Isaiah 56: 1, 6-7
"Foreigners" shall become one with the Lord.

Romans 11: 13-15, 29-32
Paul became a missionary to the "foreign" gentiles.

Matthew 15: 21-28
Jesus surrenders to the charming faith of the "foreign" woman.

Don't Be Ashamed to Charm the Lord

A boy recalls a lesson his father taught him with a handful of coins. His father threw the coins on the carpet and asked, "What did you hear?" "Nothing," the son replied. He told his son to pick up the coins and hand them to him. Then he told him to listen again. This time he threw the coins on a stone floor. "What did you hear this time?" They had naturally made a loud clatter. The father looked at his son and smiled, "My boy, always put your money where it can be heard."

In a certain sense this was the strategy used by the Canaanite woman to make herself heard by Jesus. Instead of the loud clatter of coins she employed the insistent sound of her voice backed up with a firm conviction that Jesus could and would listen to her. What makes her story appealing is the fact that she the searcher seems more diligent than Jesus the preacher.

Normally, evangelization begins with the community of believers and then spills over to outsiders. One would have expected Jesus, as preacher, to be seeking out the woman, as searcher. But there is a role reversal here, for the woman seems already to have come to faith. She is not searching for the kingdom. She wants her daughter to experience the gift of healing from the Lord of the kingdom.

The setting is the region around Tyre and Sidon, roughly present day Lebanon. The drama between Jesus and the woman is best set out like the lines in a play:

Woman: Lord, have pity on me. My daughter is troubled by a demon. (The woman is not a Jew. The apostles are embarrassed by her request. Acting like the palace guard, or a tough secretary they try to shut her up and keep her away from Christ.)

Woman: (Shouting all the louder) Lord didn't you hear me. My daughter is very sick. She's possessed.

Jesus: My mission is only to the lost sheep of the house of Israel. (This is normal evangelization strategy. Call the community of believers to conversion first. Preach and heal them first. Yet one has the uncanny feeling that Jesus seems to be using this to dodge the woman. Or is he just testing her persistence?)

Woman: (kneeling humbly) Help me, Lord. (She is not ashamed to be poor and humble and helpless before Christ.)

Jesus: It is not right to take the food of sons and daughters and throw it to the dogs. (By all standards this is a harsh and unfeeling answer, after all this is a concerned mother Jesus addresses. By sticking to a commitment only to Jews and using the Jewish word for pagans [dogs] Jesus seems to be going beyond the call of duty.)

Woman: Please Lord, even the dogs eat the leavings that fall from the master's table. (Who could resist the charm and steadfastness of this believing woman? Jesus couldn't. He admires her faith and cures her daughter.)

Jesus: Woman, you have magnificent faith! Your prayer is heard. Your daughter is cured.

At the beginning of this homily we told a story about a father who taught his son to make "his money heard." The father was teaching his son to use money as a tool of influence, perhaps even of bribery. This woman did not blackmail Jesus or bribe him. She laid before him her wounded heart and deepest needs. If this were bribery at all, it is the persuasive power of humble love. She was not buying Jesus. She was meeting him and affecting his feelings. She acted gloriously and Jesus responded splendidly. What better parable about prayer could we find?

Prayer

Lord Jesus, you were charmed by the humble frankness of the Canaanite woman and so moved to cure her daughter. We praise you for abandoning your fixed position on evangelization of the community of believers only, and thus showing us the flexibility we need when coming to terms with a wide variety of searchers for salvation. Thank you for your inspiring example and blessed be the humble woman who became the occasion of soliciting your broad based sympathy. Amen.

Twenty-first Sunday
of Ordinary Time

Isaiah 22: 15, 19-23
God gives the Key of David's House to a true leader.

Romans 11: 33-36
Peter comes to "know the mind of the Lord" as Paul did.

Matthew 16: 13-20
Jesus gives to Peter the "Keys of the Kingdom."

Jesus Establishes a Church of Stability
and Continuity

Prince Phillip built the city of Caesarea Phillipi on a majestic rock overlooking the Mediterranean sea. Phillip named the city after himself as well as the reigning Caesar, Tiberius. Phillip located the city just above the holy shrine of Pan, a god dear to Greeks and Romans. They associated Pan with fertility rites and performed sexual mating ceremonies as part of their devotion to Pan. Strong gates enclosed the shrine because Pan's power had to be contained outside the ritual times (just as sexuality needed its restraints), otherwise, there would be PAN-IC.

Christ's selection of the city on a rock by the gates of Pan was a symbolic setting almost too good to be true. Like a master dramatist Jesus chose a visual aid and stunning environment to drive home his vision of the Church and his selection of Peter to be its chief minister. The towering city on the rock will represent the stability of the Church. The gates of Pan become the gates of hell whose power will not prevail against the Church's continuity. Jesus here plans a kingdom of love, justice and mercy, a Church that will have stability and continuity.

Christ is the ultimate rock of the Church's stability and the final safeguarder of the Church's continuity. But he must find a leader to carry on his work. Such a leader must know who Christ is. This is why Jesus asks the apostles about his identity. He asks them two questions: (1) Whom do people say that I am? (2) Whom do you say that I am?

Jesus is most interested in their answer to the second question. A long silence greets his inquiry. They are not afraid of giving the wrong answer. They just do not know how to give the right answer. They love him. They admire him beyond compare. They wonder if words could be found to say who he is. Eleven of the apostles conclude that the meaning of Jesus is beyond words. Or they are too tongue tied to find words.

Peter sings the words, "You are the Messiah, the Son of the Living God!"

The unexpected richness of Peter's words dazzles us. In the light of God's fire, Peter speaks as though uttering an oracle. The words form on his lips, not from the logic of his mind, nor from the conclusions based on his observations. The learned pharisees missed the meaning of Christ. The peasant cunning of the people misread Christ. Even the intimacy the apostles shared with Christ did not bring them to the truth. Only Peter stumbled on the fact. His declaration does not flow from cold calculation or flattery. He is too innocent for such intention.

Peter's words are born in ecstasy. The blunt fisherman became the oracle of the Holy Spirit seizing his heart and informing his mind. Jesus replies as one overcome with joy and wonder. He hears the purest echo of the divine flowing through the testimony of Peter. Jesus commissions Peter: "Blest are you, Simon. No mere man has revealed this to you, but my heavenly Father. You are Rock. And on this Rock, I will build my Church. The jaws of death shall not prevail against it. I entrust to you the keys of the Kingdom of heaven."

Jesus anoints Peter the Rock to carry on his mission. Today those words "Thou art Peter . . ." may be seen at the base of the dome of St. Peter's in Rome, carved there by Michelangelo and sung by choirs to the music of Palestrina and viewed by millions. Jesus establishes by the City on the Rock and the Gates of

Pan, the Petrine Ministry, the idea that he wants a leader who will be a minister to the whole Church. That is now the role of John Paul II, and all the Popes who have been the successors to St. Peter. Let us thank God for this Petrine ministry and pray that its love and service be ever more deeply felt.

Prayer

Father, you have sent your Son Jesus to establish
a kingdom of love, justice and mercy on this
earth, in the form of a stable and continuous
Church. In the person of St. Peter, Jesus founded
a ministry for the whole Church that endures in
the popes. We thank you for this and pray that
the faith and strength of the Pope may grow and
remain firm. We ask this through Christ our
Lord, Amen.

Twenty-second Sunday of Ordinary Time

Jeremiah 20: 7-9
Jeremiah's friends mock him for his sufferings.

Romans 12: 1-2
Make the pain and death of the body a love sacrifice of healing.

Matthew 16: 21-27
Christ's friend, Peter, would stop Jesus from the Cross.

Only Love Makes Sense out of Pain and Death

Everyone likes to feel comfortable, and people will usually go out of their way to avoid discomfort. People deny death and pain. Because they deny it, they do not know what to do with it when it inevitably comes.

Take the case of the biblical Job. He lived a comfortable life. He had seven sons and three daughters. He owned a big house and a large ranch. Then tragedy struck him. Thieves came and stole his livestock. A hurricane collapsed the house where his children were having a party. They died. Lightning caused a fire in which his servants perished. Grief stricken, Job found his body covered with boils and aching sores.

People asked Job how he felt about all this. Job said, "The Lord gives. The Lord takes away. Blessed be the name of the Lord." In other words Job understood that pain and death were part of life. He never denied the possibility. But Job was unusual. Most people run away from suffering. They don't want it and don't know what to do about it when it happens.

Job found that he needed to explain pain and death to those around him, as well as he could. His wife heard him out and said, "Curse God and die." Then so-called comforters, or mourners, came to him. They decided that the only reason he is suffering is because he has sinned. After all, wicked men prosper. Why should a good man suffer? God would not allow such misery to afflict the just and obedient man. Job admits he has his faults like anyone. But he is hardly a hardened sinner.

Job stuck to his guns. To him suffering was part of life. Only love can come to terms with pain and death. Only love is stronger than the depression produced by pain and death. To the brain, pain is a frustrating puzzle and mystery. Why? Why me? Only love appreciates the healing power of accepting, admitting pain and death. Peter's brain denies death and pain for Christ. "God Forbid."

Jesus calls Peter a Satan, telling him he must face the cross, not run away from it. Any disciple of Christ must do the same. Pain without love is hell. That is why intellectuals, who are short on love, do not know what to do with pain. That is why they can justify abortions. And soon they will justify euthanasia. These are ways of running away from pain. Pain without love is hell.

Pain with love is healing. Loving parents never mind the pain it takes to raise children. The comforters of Job were right that sin is ultimately the cause of pain and death. God left people the freedom to do good and to do evil. That freedom leaves us with the choices. Many have chosen evil and spread it abroad in the world. The first sin was to disobey God. The second sin was to kill a brother. As soon as we said, "I'll do it my way, not God's way," then we were ready to kill to have our way. So sin led to death. And for centuries that network of sinning has covered the world, so much so that poets say, "Sin is in the blood."

Job was an innocent man who suffered. Jesus tells Peter he must tread the way of the cross. Jesus is an innocent man who suffered. Because Job loved God, his heart was at peace in the face of his suffering. Not that he did not anguish a bit, but was able to love to come out of his trial a better man. Logically, there was no reason for Jesus to suffer. He had done no wrong. Not only did he face pain and death, but an especially brutal and cruel one.

Can the brain explain the pain and death of Christ logically? Yes, but only after love's insight has done its work. God sent Jesus to do this because of love and affection for us, that was the divine motive. Only our faith informed love can see how this heals us and liberates us from the burden of guilt and sin. Only love is stronger than pain and death. That is the mysterious message of the Cross that Jesus addresses to Peter.

Prayer

Holy Spirit, who gives us the bravery we need in times of trial, help us to realize that the real courage arises from the insightful love you give us when we ponder the mystery of pain and death. May we realize that our minds catch on only after a faith inspired love has first coped with this mystery. Confirm our belief that love indeed is mightier than death. Amen.

Twenty-third Sunday of Ordinary Time

Ezekiel 33: 7-9
Speak out to the man in conflict with God. Help him change.

Romans 13: 8-10
Christian conflict is part of growing in love.

Matthew 18: 15-20
Jesus offers a plan for meeting conflict.

"Christian" Conflict Is an Occasion to Make Love Grow

A husband and a wife were having a continuing argument about who really runs the family. Each one insisted it was the other. One night, the husband joyfully announced, "Dear, I have finally proved that you're the boss." Holding a copy of a women's magazine, he said, "I took this test, and it proves that you are the dominant one in this family."

The wife looked at the magazine and said, "There are separate tests here for males and females. how could you have come up with my results? I haven't taken the test." Without missing a beat, the husband shamelessly said, "Oh, I know how you think. So I just looked over the questions and answered them for you."

This gentle and mildly humorous anecdote about a mild form of rivalry and conflict in a marriage may serve as a starter for looking at Christ's words about conflict management in the Gospel. Christ follows a slow, careful, conservative plan for solving personality conflicts—or other kinds of conflicts for that matter. Jesus counsels sensitivity and discretion. First, let it be a purely private matter. Then bring in a good friend to act as arbiter. Lastly, bring the case to the attention of a wider community. Only after all this, in the face of complete intransigence, does Jesus advise excluding the offender from the community.

Jesus does not spell out any strategy for how the parties should handle the conflict, other than to speak of deepening stages of involvement on the part of others. Perhaps some comments on that can put some flesh and bones on the outline he offers.

Conflict is part of life, just like death and taxes. In itself conflict is neither good nor bad. But conflict can be valuable for deepening love if it is handled well. Many people find it hard to handle conflict. They avoid it. They pretend it doesn't exist. Or they dig in and slug it out. Generally, people practice either fight or flight. But this often intensifies the conflict.

If the parties to conflict are committed to a "win-lose" situation, then someone has to lose or give in, causing bitterness and humiliation in the loser. If they can give themselves to a "win-win" situation, then love deepens as each party gives up the desire to control the other. In any conflict we should try to find out which of these attitudes prevail in the conflicting people. So, the situation needs to be evaluated. What are some guidelines that may help?

(1) Get the persons to express their feelings and needs without talking of solutions.

(2) Propose a variety of solutions without settling on any one of them.

(3) After a host of solutions have been mentioned, put a value on each, noting the advantages and disadvantages.

(4) Get the persons to agree on one of the solutions.

(5) Make them say how they will go about solving the problem, and set a date for starting and a first evaluation.

(6) Meet with them to see how things are going.

It takes a long time to develop a serious conflict. It takes just as long a time to solve one. Love needs time to work and be reactivated. Patience on the part of friends and counselors is of the essence. Also a positive attitude in the face of some tense situations is needed. Some people think that conflict is un-Christian. So they hide from it.

But conflict is just a fact. It only becomes non-Christian when the parties lack the courage and faith to face the conflict and do something about it. Conflict is an occasion for growth in love. Let's make sure that occasion is used to the best advantage.

Prayer

Jesus, in calling us to love one another, you were well aware of how much conflict arises in human relationships. Rightly you advise us to face the conflict in a loving and sympathetic manner. You also caution us to go slowly and in stages in the effort to find a solution. Abide with us as we face our personal conflicts and assist us to achieve a "win-win" situation. Amen.

Twenty-fourth Sunday of Ordinary Time

Sirach 27: 30; 28: 7
Forgive your neighbor's injustice.

Romans 14: 7-9
We are not our own masters, but servants of God.

Matthew 18: 21-35
Contrast the merciless servant to the merciful God.

Forgiveness: The Gentle Rain from Heaven

A few years ago, an eleven year old boy woke up as usual and began dressing for school. As he listened to the morning news, he froze. United Air Lines, flight 629, with forty-four persons aboard, had exploded and crashed. The boy rushed downstairs to find his grandmother, who was talking quietly with the parish priest. "Mom and dad were on that plane, weren't they?" Someone had placed a bomb on that plane.

Later that morning the students at the parish school asked for a prayer service. The pastor asked the boy if it would be all right with him and his brothers. The boy agreed and said, "Would they please say a prayer for the man who killed my mom and dad?" Like the Lord who forgave those who brutalized him at Calvary, this young boy expressed the divine and noble sentiment of forgiveness in his hour of deepest personal grief.

Shakespeare says that the quality of mercy cannot be strained. Genuine forgiveness may never be diluted by feelings of revenge, resentment or anger. Kings are supposed to be noted for their capacity to dispense justice, but mercy becomes the throned monarch better than his crown.

Forgiveness makes everyone better than their status of parent, president or principal. Too many families and friendships are torn apart because the principle of forgiveness is ignored or forgotten. Instead of forgiving, people choose to nourish presumably justified anger about the fault of the one who did the injury. Yet the old axiom, forget and forgive still stands. Alexander Pope writes:

> "Teach me to feel another's woe,
> To hide the fault I see.
> That mercy I to others show
> That mercy show to me."*

---

*From *The International Dictionary of Thoughts*, edited by John Bradley, Chicago: Ferguson, 1969, page 482.

Today's readings celebrate mercy and forgiveness, that attribute of awe and majesty. Sirach says that only sinners hug tight the hateful qualities of wrath and unforgiving anger. He advises us to forgive our neighbor's injustice. Paul tells the Romans that we are not our own final masters, but ultimately servants of the Lord, the true master who never ceases to forgive. Jesus tells the story of the unforgiving servant to remind his listeners of the tragedy of the merciless heart.

Poets and philosophers tend to make forgiveness a divine value because it is so often lacking in humans: To err is human, to be unforgiving is human, to forgive is divine. Forgiveness comes hard to many people because they spend too much time licking their own wounds and examining the motives of the injuring party. It is unfortunately too easy to find reasons to justify maintaining a hard line against those who have hurt us. Yet Christ advises us to see that the wound is not in ourselves, but in the one who wounded us. The real wound is in the wounder. The capacity to heal is in the one wounded. Forgiveness is the gentle rain that blesses him or her who gives and the one who receives. It causes the growth of new and richer friendship.

In spiteful arguments the contestants strive to have the last word. Forgiveness is one way to speak that word. Or seen from the other side, an apology is a good way to have the last word.

Prayer

Father of mercies, your boundless capacity to
forgive is both a model and cause of our own
hopes both to receive mercy and bestow it. Your
gracious power has shown endless signs of mercy
in the past. May we today experience it once
more as we resolve to forget and forgive real and
imagined slights and offenses. Amen.

Twenty-fifth Sunday of Ordinary Time

Isaiah 55: 6-9
Bring in the scoundrel to feel the power of God's love.

Philippians 1: 20-24, 27
Paul is torn between living for his brethren or dying to be with Christ.

Matthew 20: 1-16
The grape pickers must learn the generosity of God.

The Grape Pickers Must Love as Outrageously as God

An Irish parable tells the story of a storm that ravaged a set of farms. Afterwards at the pub, Pat moaned and groaned about losing his house. A buddy said, "Did you hear what happened to Mike?" "No." "He lost his house AND his barn." A contented smile crossed Pat's face. "There, I feel better now." Pat felt pleased because he was better off than Mike.

In reading the parable of the grape pickers, an eighth grader said, "If the grape pickers who started at dawn had not known the salary given to those at the eleventh hour, they would have gone home happy. Why is it that some people's happiness depends on feeling better off than others?"

Several reasons come to mind. Other people's misfortunes give us a sense of relief at our own good fortune. "There, but for the grace of God go I." Another reason could be that our idea of justice is confined to contracts and exact measuring. That means there is a bit of the child in all of us. If our brother gets a bigger piece of the pie, a twinge of jealousy picks at us. A lot of us still walk around with the child very much alive in our adult bodies. Our mouths are always open to be fed. Yet as adults we should be looking to see how to feed others.

Christ's parable of the grape pickers has the same message as his story of the prodigal son and his forgiveness of the good thief on the cross. In each case someone is made unhappy by generosity shown. The elder brother takes offense at the fuss made over his younger brother. "He's been fooling around for years, while I stayed home and worked hard. He doesn't deserve all those hugs, kisses and parties. I do. He should be made to suffer for his sins."

Similarly, the grape pickers who have worked all day gripe about the generosity of the vine manager who gives the eleventh hour workers the same salary. "They don't deserve a full salary. They didn't work for it. We did." And on the cross, the bad thief curses Christ. The Good thief blesses him and attains paradise. To some, his "death-bed" conversion on the cross is offensive. He didn't work hard enough for paradise, for the full salary.

Jesus is trying to say that no one can work hard enough for heaven. Heaven is not something we earn by the sweat of our brow. Heaven is a gift of love from God. The rules in the game of divine grace are not the same as human rules of contract. God loves outrageously and asks us to have as big a heart. Jesus spoke of bad scandal, as when an adult scandalizes a child. "Better that a millstone be hung around the neck of such a person than to scandalize a child." In this parable Jesus speaks of good scandal in which God scandalizes good people. God flaunts his love and dares his followers to catch up and match it.

The lesson of the parable of the Grape Pickers is similar to that of the Lost Sheep. Jesus focuses on the sheer delight one should have at bringing a lost soul home to the kingdom of love. The hard working grape pickers, like the elder brother, already enjoy the wealth of the kingdom. They are spiritually rich. Why be small minded and begrudge the affection lavished on the lost sheep?

No one is forgetting the fidelity of the saved. God is simply giving a party to a newcomer in our midst. Jesus is reminding us of how rich we are in love. We can afford to give much because we have received much.

Don't make morality a contract. Let our relationships be as big as our hearts full of love. We do not need to be happy at the expense of someone else's misery. Our happiness comes from knowing we are loved without reserve. Our happiness increases when we throw a party for a newcomer to our community of love.

Prayer

Holy Spirit, we need the insight of the parable of the Grape Pickers, because we tend to be petty in our relationship with one another. Too often we are childishly jealous when we should be maturely generous. Expand our hearts with love that we may take in the newcomers to the kingdom with a huge welcome. Teach us how to love as you do. Never let us seek happiness at the expense of other's misery. Amen.

Twenty-sixth Sunday of Ordinary Time

Ezekiel 18: 25-28
Good men may only seem virtuous. Bad men can really change.

Philippians 2: 1-11
Jesus was obedient unto death, and now is Lord.

Matthew 21: 28-32
Jesus contrasts lip service with performance.

Lip Service Versus Performance

St. Louis IX, King of France, was known to be a wise and witty man. Take the case of how he handled the Farmer's Turnip. A poor farmer had a good turnip crop. He celebrated his good fortune by selecting the biggest turnip as a gift for the king. He came to the palace and stood in a long line, awaiting his turn to meet the king and present his gift.

Finally he arrived at the throne and offered his present. Louis was charmed. "Bring me a scale, " said Louis. When the scale was brought, the king said, "Give this man the turnip's weight in gold." The poor farmer left the king's presence walking on air, with a heart full of joy.

The king's act prompted some of his courtiers to reflect. What might the king do for them, if they gave him presents? A week later, a rich man came to the king and gave him his finest horse as a gift. The king looked at the horse and smiled. "Thank you. I will put this horse in my stable and look forward to riding him. Such a fine horse." Then turning to his servant he said, "Give this man the turnip!"

The rich men around the king were "yes men," choked with self-interest. They were big on lip service and short on performance. They told the king what he liked to hear. The king realized that the day he was crowned, he would never again eat a bad meal, read a good book—or hear the truth.

The poor farmers, who lived far from the king, were normally "no men." They grumbled about taxes and complained about the laws. Yet they were short on flattery and long on service. They did their jobs. The "yes men" excelled at lip service. The "no men" could be counted on for performance. That was why the farmer's turnip was worth its weight in gold. And why the rich man's horse was worth hardly more than a turnip.

In the reading from Matthew, Christ's story of the two sons dramatizes the difference between lip service and sound performance. One son said he would obey his father, but he didn't.

The second son refused to obey, but on reflection, did do what his father told him. Who was the greater man? Who was truly committed to the father?

The apostles agreed it was the second son, the "no man." Jesus applied the story to the externally religious, who say all the right prayers and attend all the services, and even contribute to the right charities. But behind all this they are doing their own thing. They are not necessarily doing the will of the father. Moreover, their intentions are spoiled by their hypocrisy and the self-righteousness.

Jesus sides with the sinners, like the whores and tax collectors. They have a more likely chance of finding the kingdom of heaven. They have a truer estimation of their real state in life. They know they are sinners. The trouble with hypocrites is that they think they are holy whereas in fact they are sinning by their judgmentalism. Sinners are told often enough that they are unholy. They are not likely to forget who they are. Knowing who they are they have a chance to change when faced with a forgiving and loving invitation. People who think they have it made have closed their minds and so are hard to convert.

Some school teachers say, "I would rather work with bad students than the goody two shoes." Somehow it seems more fulfilling to work with students who grumble and say no. The challenge for them is clearer and the possibility of bringing them around to performance is higher. Whereas to have a class of students who seem agreeable and apparently cooperative, is sometimes to face a group that is subtly resisting everything you try to make them perform.

Now, of course, none of this means we should all become bad in order to be good. It does mean that if we think we are good, "yes men and women" before God, then we must be darn sure we are more than "lip servers." We must be performers.

Prayer

Father in heaven, you must hear many a yes
coming from us, but look in vain for
performance. Then you hear many a no, but find
a conversion among the sinners. Give us the
insight into ourselves to see how easily we can
deceive ourselves with our yes, but never do
anything. Strengthen us to make the yes of our
mouth be an act of our whole person. Amen.

Twenty-seventh Sunday of Ordinary Time

Isaiah 5: 1-7
God's loving care for his vineyard Israel—their ingratitude.

Philippians 4: 6-9
Paul lists some gospel values for the Philippians.

Matthew 21: 33-43
Jesus repeats the Isaiah parable and its meaning.

Divine Caring—Human Indifference

France and California boast about their fine wines and the
painstaking care they bestow on the vineyards that yield the
grapes. Biblical Palestine was no less proud of its vineyards.
When Moses planned an entry into Palestine, he sent scouts to
see what the land was like. Numbers 13:23 reports that the scouts

returned with bunches of grapes so heavy that it took two men to bear them on a staff between them. They found them in the Brook of Eschol, which means the Valley of the Grapes. Even today that valley is rich in grapes. Heavy bunches weighing ten to twelve pounds are no rarity.

The soil of biblical Palestine favored the growth of grapes. Vines flourished on high stone walled terraces as at Samaria. They also did well on the lowlands in areas such as the plains of Jericho and Esdraelon. Early Israelites, coming in from the deserts, saw the vine shaded homes of the local inhabitants. They yearned for a time when they also would sit under their own vine and fig tree. The descriptions of the vineyards and the hazards of protecting them in today's readings are realistic accounts well known to anyone in the grape growing business of biblical times.

So prevalent were the vineyards, and so well known the vine growers' problems that Jesus could easily use vineyard stories to explain religious truths because his listeners knew the situations well. The growing popularity of wine in the United States and the ease of travel is familiarizing Americans with the vineyards of California and New York and even the wine country of France.

One thing that all grape growers know, and tourists come to know, is the vigilant care needed to produce good grapes. If ever the word *cultivation* could assume its proper sense it is in the area of grape growing. As in any human endeavor there are bound to be disappointments, the ones that can occur in vineyards are all the more shattering because so much has been invested in terms of money, time and personal involvement. Few pursuits in life demand more intense attention than the cultivation of a first class vineyard. One need only add then the equal attention given to the production of the wine that ensues.

Christ's sermons about the vineyard would make just as much sense today in the Napa Valley or in the fields of Burgundy, where so much loving care is sometimes attended by cruel disappointment. As Jesus would put it, however, no grape grower could be more exhaustive in his loving care for a vineyard as God is for the Church and for the people whom He is trying to shape into a harvest worthy of a divine destiny. As Jesus would put it, no grape grower's disappointment over a bad batch of grapes could match the divine disappointment over an ungrateful and sinful outgrowth of the processes of divine cultivation. Just as a vintner cannot force the final product so neither can God force saintliness. How similar is the case of parents who do so much for their children only to face, tragically, a disappointing outcome in the end. The mystery of freedom and the possibility of choosing evil can produce the sour grapes that frustrate the final purpose of God.

But the same freedom that moves us to evil can bring us to grace. God creates a social environment by grace that can help us surmount all temptations to self-destructive evil. Our sensitivity to this banishes the dead end of the grapes of wrath and instead calls for a wine festival begun at Eucharist and completed in the kingdom of heaven.

Prayer

Holy Spirit, the words of scripture often speak of
your coming in terms of great torrents of good
wine. As we ponder the divine care that is
illustrated by the cultivation of a vineyard, may
we know in you the grace to be responsive and
grateful for this constant guidance. In abiding
with us, help us to overcome indifference and
rather yearn to be alert with expressions of
thankfulness. Amen.

Twenty-eighth Sunday of Ordinary Time

Isaiah 25: 6-10
God prepares a banquet for us on His holy mountain.

Philippians 4: 12-14, 19-20
Christ is the ultimate banquet of our souls.

Matthew 22: 1-14
Jesus uses a wedding banquet to symbolize the kingdom.

Be Sure to "Dress Up" for the Kingdom Banquet

In Old Testament times, weddings began at the groom's tent and then moved to the banquet table and dance floor. Bridesmaids led the veiled and bejeweled bride to the tent of the groom where the marriage rite was performed. By Christ's time, the wedding ceremony was changed from the groom's tent to the outdoors, where a canopy was held over the heads of the happy couple. If the canopy was not fixed to the ground, it was held by four unmarried young men. The two mothers lead the bride to the ritual canopy. The two fathers escorted the groom.

All the features of a good party followed the wedding rite: feasting, dancing, story telling and even the use of riddles, as in the story of Samson (Judges 14: 10-20). Just as in our own day, there was a concern then about a plentiful supply of food and drink. The Cana story is an example of a depleted wine supply, which Mary sought to solve in her plea to Jesus.

Normally, personal couriers were sent as messengers to invite people to the marriage. The inviters expected the invited to come. Refusal was considered an insult, unless there were demonstrably good excuses. In today's gospel, the refusers do more than insult the king; they abuse and even kill his messengers.

The hosts had every right to expect that the guests dress properly for the party. In biblical times, the grooms often provided textiles for the guests, so they could fashion proper robes and gowns for the wedding. Small wonder the hosts were offended when guests arrived improperly clad. It may be chic, in some cases, to arrive today in blue jeans for a wedding, but normally, formal attire is expected. It is not unknown today that an offensive guest be asked to leave the party. We can sympathize with the king of today's parable. He had enough trouble with his guest list. Having someone who decided to "dress down" for the wedding, simply added injury to insult.

Jesus uses the story to illustrate his kingdom of love, justice and mercy. He scores three points.

1. The self-complacent will refuse the kingdom. A wedding party signifies much that is best about all of us: consecrated love, abundance of food, joyful dancing and hearty story-telling. Christ's kingdom is just such a community of love and human fulfillment. To make it work, people must join in the give and take of community living and loving. The self-complacent only want to take. They do not want to give. They "shall be as gods." So they kill off the possibilities of love, justice and mercy.

2. The poor, blind and lame accept the kingdom. People who need love, *and know they need it,* are the luckiest people. These are the people who realize they must take love in order to give it. They reach out to have love conferred upon them, so they will have love to share at Christ's wedding party. They do not take in order to hoard. They take so they can give. That is why they joyfully accept the kingdom. They are poor, blind and lame, until transformed by love.

3. One must "dress up" for the kingdom. The groom provided the material of love for the wedding garment of outgoing affection to be showered on others at the party. Those who took the love, but did not want to

share it, have missed the point. They will not wear outside the garment of love, concern and mercy. They will hold it selfishly in their grubby palms and not give it to others. They cannot be true members of the wedding/kingdom. What does this say to us? (a) Banish your self-complacency. (b) Know your need for love. (c) "Dress up" by giving the love you have received. We all know that weddings are happy events. Life in Christ's kingdom is even happier.

Prayer

Jesus we praise you for asking us to "dress up" for the kingdom banquet. We plead for the grace that will eliminate our self-complacency, an insight that moves us to stand with the poor in spirit and an ability to share the love received from you. Caution us never to "dress down" in our plans for membership in your kingdom. Amen.

Twenty-ninth Sunday of Ordinary Time

Isaiah 45: 1, 4-6
God uses the politician Cyrus for a religious purpose.

1 Thessalonians 1: 1-5
Paul praises the faith of the Thessalonians.

Matthew 22: 15-21
Jesus uses a tax issue to awaken awareness of God.

From a Tax Issue to God Awareness

Put your hand on someone's wallet and you are probably in for trouble. Not everyone would agree with Shakespeare's Iago when he says, "Who steals my purse steals trash. But he that filches from me my good name makes me poor indeed." People may worry about their good name, but they are liable to worry just as much about their wallets. All the more so, when the tax agents have their eye on it.

It has been said that "Nothing is as certain as death and taxes." Tax issues do not always bring out the best in our characters. Will Rogers once said, "The income tax has made more liars out of Americans than gold has." Unfair taxes rile the tempers of citizens, as happened in the case of the Boston Tea Party—a protest against British taxes.

The Jews of Christ's time hated taxes with a passion, mainly because they had to pay them to a hated oppressor, the Roman government. Rome provoked even greater anger because she taxed so close to the bone. Jews could well agree with Mortimer Caplin's dictum, "There is one difference between a tax collector and a taxidermist. The taxidermist leaves the hide." Rome forgot that in levying taxes and shearing sheep, it is well to stop when you get down to the skin.

There was plenty of evidence of Roman taxation. The Roman census, that caused Mary and Joseph to journey to Bethlehem, was designed to figure out the tax base in Palestine. Romans imposed taxes on water, meat, salt and property. Tax collectors, like Matthew, gathered fees on all exports at border towns. Pilgrims had to pay road tolls. No topic could unleash explosive anger more than a discussion of taxes. No question placed to Jesus could be more intimidating.

Two groups place the tax question to Jesus: the Herodians, who favor appeasing Rome and paying the taxes, and the Pharisees, who hate Rome and heatedly oppose the taxes. The Herodians don't like Christ because they see him as upsetting the balance of power. The Pharisees dislike Christ because he is not political enough. He does not seem sufficiently interested in political liberation from Rome. Both groups want Jesus to declare his political position on taxes. But Christ's primary interest is in the acceptance of the spiritual kingdom of God. Solving political questions is not his immediate goal.

"Is it lawful to pay tax to the emperor?"

Jesus replies astutely. He exposes their motivations.

(1) You hypocrites; Jesus exposes their pretended innocence. They are not open to his opinion or teaching. They want to trap him and get him into trouble.

(2) To the godless Herodians, Jesus says that tribute should be paid to God. He basically tells them they have sold their religion out for Roman kickbacks. They have reduced religion to politics for their own self-interest. Give unto God!

(3) To the presumably godly Pharisees, Jesus says that tribute should be paid to Caesar. He basically tells them they are just as godless as the Herodians, because they want a political solution to what is basically a spiritual problem. Were they truly seeking God's kingdom, they would not be choosing the wrong solution to their dilemma. Give unto Caesar!

Jesus removes the answer from the realm of politics and puts it in the arena of personal conscience. He does not offer them a political theory. He takes no partisan position on politics. He does take a position on personal conscience. He sees them as politicians without God. He wants them to begin with God's kingdom and then come to grips with other issues. He evades the political question to confront them with the spiritual one. It's so easy to argue about taxes. It is far more difficult to open oneself to God.

That is fairly true of ourselves as well.

Prayer

Lord, touch our powers of discrimination so that
we do not mistake spiritual for political goals.
Open our minds to see that many would have us
reduce all human problems to the political arena
and involve us in the fights that attend this
vision. Alert us to realize that our principal
concern is the spiritual and that all else must be
judged in the light of faith that proceeds from
involvement in such an outlook. Amen.

Thirtieth Sunday
of Ordinary Time

Exodus 22: 20-26
Treat people justly.

1 Thessalonians 1: 5-10
Become a model for believers.

Matthew 22: 34-40
Learn the law of love.

An Abundance of Love

Parade Magazine reported not long ago about the continuance
of a Mexican version of Boys Town, known as *Hogar Infantil.*
Founded by an American named Nich (pronounced Nick) Andersen, the ranch for poor and orphaned boys provides them
with nourishment and education. The secret of its success is the
abundance of love Nich possessed and the legacy of love passed
onto Jorge Hernandez, the new head of Hogar Infantil.

Nich was a father who could forgive and forget. Jorge recalls the story of a nine-year-old orphan who felt he had enough of the ranch and decided to make it on his own in the world. For three years the boy worked the streets, finding a job here and there, curling up in a doorway at night, scratching for what food he could find. Eventually, the hardship crushed him. Barely able to walk, he returned to the ranch. When Nich saw the boy, he did not scold or rebuke him. He folded the boy in his arms and wept.

An abundance of love in the hearts of men like Nich Andersen has produced the miracle that is *Hogar Infantil.* The Roman poet Terence wrote that , "It is possible for a man to be so changed by love as hardly to be recognized as the same person." The marvel of love is that the more you expend it on others the more you acquire. Everything else disappears in the use. Tires wear out. Bodies age and wither. Roads crack in the winter and air conditioners collapse in summer. The strings of a tennis racket snap and the threads of a softball unwind. Felt pens dry up and washing machine motors grind to a halt.

The supreme pleasure of love is that its use causes more love. It is the only investment that never knows a recession. The Greek myth about King Midas claimed that everything he touched turned to gold. While love may not always be successful in transforming the object of its affections, its batting average is so high that no other way of human improvement can match it.

Today's liturgy celebrates the law of love. Jesus tells us that the foundation of all morality and ethics is love. The first reading outlines ways to show love. The second reading declares that loving behavior is the only way to be a model for believers and unbelievers alike. The third reading enunciates the love principle that undergirds all religion and moral endeavor.

We all know that we are acquisitive by nature. We pile up wealth and possessions and then pay a lot of money to secure and guard them. We fear their loss. Yet the greatest treasure and gold is free, namely, our capacity to love. Each time we love we increase our power to love. The treasure room of our hearts grows far greater than Fort Knox or a Swiss bank account. It will cost us no money to secure it and we find that love put to use never wears out the virtue we are acquiring.

Wouldn't it be wiser then to spend our days increasing our capacity to love? Why not take our avaricious nature and its hungers and desires and put them to the service of love? For almost all other acquisitions we need to go somewhere—to the store, to another city, to the moon for that matter. To begin to love we need go nowhere further than our own hearts and personal freedom. Each time we empty our hearts with affection for another, we paradoxically have a fuller heart. It takes a small effort to start. The proof of this pudding is in the doing. Begin today. Then you will enjoy all the happiness of the world. You will have lived and loved.

Prayer

Spirit of love, with your intimate presence
within our hearts we have a fair chance of
learning the law of love. Wake up our minds to
the plain truth that practicing love increases
love. Show us that this talent is so close at hand
that nothing need separate us from being loving
people. We praise you for this and thank you for
your overflowing love. Amen.

Feast of All Saints

Revelation 7: 2-4, 9-14
A heavenly vision of the saints in light.

1 John 3: 1-3
Saints are very much like Christ.

Matthew 5: 1-12
Saints embody the meaning of the beatitudes.

Bring Back the Saints

It's time to bring back the saints. We need those cheerful, outrageous, inspiring, frustrating and courageous men and women both as good examples and intercessors for us.

We need the humanity of St. Peter. Impulsive, inadequate, repentant, he helps us feel we can be saints too. Manly and protective, he assures Christ that no one will harm him while Peter is around. And then Peter cannot even face down a chatty woman who accuses him of being Christ's friend. A fisherman used to storms, Peter screams in fear when he sinks in the waves after asking Christ to bid him walk across the waters. He let his best friend down, but he was humble enough to cry about it and ask forgiveness. In the end he became the Prince of Apostles.

We need the passion of St. Paul. There are over two billion people in this world who have not accepted Christ. Up in heaven, Paul must be pacing the floors wishing he were here to roam the world calling people to the love and forgiveness of Christ. Paul's passion for Christ was born in deep prayer. He spent three years in contemplation in the Arabian desert. There he felt the ecstasy of God in his "third heaven" experience. He also knew the "thorn in the flesh," the necessary Cross that goes with our Easters. After two weeks with Peter in Jerusalem he agreed to four more years in solitude. His ministry of silence in Tarsus helped him soak up more of the *soul power* from God that he would need for converting the world to Christ. Then he was ready to sail forth and conquer the world for Christ. We need Peter's humanity and Paul's passion for Christ.

We need the humor of a Phillip Neri. He wanted to dispel the idea that saints should be solemn. To this end he strolled around Rome wearing his clothes inside out, along with floppy white shoes. When he heard that people thought him humble, he borrowed a friend's mink cloak. He paraded with it in public, posturing vainly and acting like a snob. The child and clown in Phillip led him to shave only half his beard, or walk around with a cushion on his head. He wanted to make people laugh. To him laughter was the best medicine. Laughter is next to godliness. Yet he was no fool. He discovered Palestrina and started polyphonic music for the Church. He fostered the study of scientific Church history. Lastly, he founded an Order of prayerful intellectuals, the most famous of whom was England's Cardinal Newman.

We need the gutsiness of Catherine of Siena. One of the worst problems of the fourteenth century was the Avignon Papacy. The king of France controlled the Pope. Corruption flowered in the papal court. Bishops and priests were second rate men. A thirty-year-old laywoman, Catherine of Siena, felt called to go to Avignon and persuade the Pope to reform the Church and take the papacy back to Rome. Deeply prayerful and marvelously outgoing, Catherine spent four months negotiating, pleading, and cajoling the Pope until she won the day. She changed the mind of the Pope and changed the course of history. She knew how to be both a contemplative and a politician in the same breath. She had guts.

Bring back the saints. On this feast of All Saints we should resolve to bring back the saints into our lives. We should not allow the message of this generation to dominate our religion. The "Now People" think they have nothing to learn from history. The trouble with "Now People" is that they very soon become "Then People." The individual who marries the spirit of an age soon becomes a widower. The parade of the saints reminds us of how Christ is made present in history and how we can contribute our own part. Bring in the saints. God knows we have enough sinners around.

Prayer

Father of the heavenly realm, we praise you for
the victory of the saints into whom you poured
so much love and grace. May we join our hymns
of joy to those of the saints who offer you
grateful canticles for the ultimate fulfillment
they find in you. In communion with the saints
we trust that we will both be inspired to follow
their example as well as to benefit from their
intercessory prayers for us. Amen.

Thirty-first Sunday
of Ordinary Time

Malachi 2: 8-9
God rebukes the clergy for misleading the people.

1 Thessalonians 2: 7-9, 13
Paul says a good leader is like a good mother.

Matthew 23: 1-10
Jesus rebukes religious leaders for hypocrisy.

Bad Religious Leaders

Biblical and Church history abound with accounts about bad religious leaders. We all know how much corruption in Church leadership led to the Reformation. What are some reasons for the debasement of Church leadership from time to time? One way of looking at it is that money and sex seem to bring out the worst in people—and all the more so in religious leaders. The combination of avarice and lust on the eve of the Reformation was reducing Christendom to a shambles. The princely life-styles of Churchmen required heaping amounts of money to maintain their households. Sexual laxity eroded the ideals of celibacy.

Plain old-fashioned greed seems to be the devil in most cases. Nothing dramatized this more than the sale of indulgences at the time of the Reformation. Often the quantity of the indulgence was based on both the ability to pay as well as the impressiveness of the saint's relic used to motivate the sale.

Take, for example, the fund raising campaign in Germany for money to build St. Peter's Basilica. Archbishop Albrecht of Mainz drew from a collection of 9,000 relics such tropies as: bodies of saints, one of Isaac's bones, a piece of manna, a branch from the burning bush of Moses, one of the Cana jars, a thorn from Christ's crown, a body of one of the Holy Innocents and one of the stones that killed St. Stephen. Most of these relics were spurious fakes, but that did not deter either seller or buyer. The scandal was strong enough to move Luther to set in motion the forces of the Reformation.

Today's readings record some strong biblical language directed against bad religious leaders. Malachy reports God using words like these: "I will send a curse upon you . . . I hold you in contempt." Jesus indicts the hypocrisy of the religious leaders of his time with biting accuracy as he outlines their crimes and sins. The only breather we have in today's liturgy is in reading two where Paul says a good religious leader is like a good mother. "While we were among you, we were as gentle as any mother fondling her little ones."

Contemporary culture poses serious threats to the integrity of today's religious leaders. As in every other age, sex and money, backed up by attitudes of avarice and lust are the hounds that bite at the heels of religious leaders—and of course all other leadership as well. Maybe it will be only avarice and not lust. Maybe it will be just lust and not avarice. No matter, either passion can ruin an individual.

The secular press speaks of credibility gaps, a fancy way of describing hypocrisy based on greed. It is perhaps no mistake that the major political scandals of the last decade have been those arising from misuse of money and sex, leading to lies and hypocrisy and venality. Religious leaders are as human as anyone else and prone to infection by the evil signs of the times. It happened before, in biblical kingdoms, in New Testament times and in the age preceding the Reformation.

Today's liturgy raises caution signals for religious leaders to examine their motives and honesty and integrity. The flocks are to be led by Good Shepherds, not wolves. Failures in leadership, whether religious, political or parental are almost always due to a capitulation to passions that wreck sincerity and the attitudes of open and blameless behavior. "Take heed lest ye fall" is the lesson leaping out at us today. History is full of such falls. They need not be repeated in our time. As Paul says, a good leader is like a good mother.

Prayer

Lord God, you have expressed sentiments of
judgment against bad religious leaders. You
know how avarice and lust and other passions
can make them unfaithful leaders of your people.
Guard us from ever submitting to such drives
and thus from betraying your people. We pray
for the grace to be leaders of integrity. Amen.

Thirty-second Sunday
of Ordinary Time

Wisdom 6: 12-16
Divine wisdom never disappoints its users.

1 Thessalonians 4: 13-18
Divine wisdom evokes faith in eternal life.

Matthew 25: 1-13
Divine wisdom tempers human foolishness.

Divine Wisdom and Human Folly

A fool and his money are soon parted. What fools these mor-
tals be! A fool can ask more questions than a wise man can answer. Such sayings characterize the prevalence of human folly.
Take the case of John who keeps passing up gas stations even
though his gauge tells him his tank is less than a quarter full.
All of sudden, empty! And no gas station in sight. "How stupid
of me," he says.

Or think of the Smiths who want a new home in a certain price range. They save up for the right down payment and set out to find their dream house. In the meantime they see a boat for sale and can't resist buying it. A week later they see the house they want, but their down payment is gone. By the time they accumulate another block of cash, inflation has put their dream house well beyond their means. They curse their foolishness.

The French army of the second world war lamented the folly of the Maginot Line where the guns could only point one way. Old line German strategists complained about the foolishness of Hitler invading Russia and so fighting a war on two fronts. As the Spanish proverb puts it, "What the fool does at the end is what the wise man does at the beginning." And the psalms tell us, "The fool says in his heart, ' There is no God.' " (Psalms 14:1)

Today's readings contrast divine wisdom and human foolishness. Sirach says that wisdom never disappoints its users, especially because its eternal viewpoint provides the long range view that helps forestall impetuous foolishness. Paul tells the Thessalonians who are foolishly worried about the imminent end of the world that divine wisdom would teach them that eternal life is already experienced here as well as after death. The bodies of those already dead will indeed rise again.

Jesus praises the wise virgins over the foolish ones because their spiritual foresight won for them the experience of God's kingdom.

Both human prudence and divine wisdom operate on the principle that forewarned is forearmed. If the gas tank is practically empty the foolish birdesmaids will be late for the wedding. In like manner if the fund of spiritual resources is depleted the believer may not make it to God, or be of much use to one's neighbor either. Human prudence realizes that proper planning is the best way to avoid foolish mistakes. Haste not only makes waste but folly as well.

Divine wisdom infuses the mind with a sense of the eternal in time. It stretches short-sightedness into the long view, a perspective not limited by the edge of one's nose. Hence the believer both benefits from the serenity that a depth view affords and enjoys the divine support for human practicality. Divine wisdom helps the believer slow down the rapid flow of the passing parade so that one has the strength to make some sensible judgments about the meaning of the flow of events.

Divine wisdom does not assure the believer that he or she will never make a mistake or do something foolish. That would assume a perfection not found this side of paradise. But it does assert it will save us from being fools. It cleans out our ears to hear the great words, "The groom is here! Christ has come! Greet him and join him!" You will, won't you? Amen.

Prayer

O Divine Wisdom, source of all human prudence,
infuse within our minds the long range view
that proceeds from the eternal perspective. Thus
may we act wisely in our spiritual lives and
prudently in our human affairs. Amen.

Thirty-third Sunday of Ordinary Time

Proverbs 31: 1-13, 19-20, 30-31
The wife who uses all her skills.

I Thessalonians 5: 1-6
Wake up and use all your talents.

Matthew 25: 14-30
Use your skills and soul power, or you will lose it.

Use Your Soul Power, Or Lose Your Soul

Use it or lose it! That is the message to anyone who wants better muscles in his or her body, or better brain power.

Take the story of the crushing news a teenager once brought to his parents. They had wanted their son to be a bright boy and get a good education. Instead they bred a boy who was slow in the primary grades and troublesome in the intermediate ones. Now he comes home to tell them that his high school had expelled him. Later he wrote about that experience, "My intellectual development was slow. I did not begin to wonder about time and space until I was an adult." The result? Eleven years after being thrown out of school, this boy—Albert Einstein—published the theory of relativity. The "slow boy" changed our view of the universe.

He may have been slow, but he never stopped using his mind. **Use it or lose it.** Doubtless he had native genius. But he testifies that much of his secret lay in the fact that he ceaselessly used his mind. He loved playing games with ideas and was dogged in developing his ability to do so.

Would you think there was much of a future for the following man? He is fifty-three years old. Virtually all his life he has fought a losing battle against debt and misfortune. He lost the use of his left hand in a war injury. He tried several government jobs and succeeded at none of them. He spent many a month in jail. Despite all these defeats and failures, he feels the drive to write a book. Seldom has a book been more wildly successful. For over 350 years his book has captivated and charmed countless thousands of people. The prisoner was Cervantes. The book was *Don Quixote*.

When virtually all his peers were preparing for death, or in fact dead, Cervantes erupted into a fountain of creativity that left a permanent mark on literature. Why didn't he run out of steam like most people do?

Cervantes never let his imagination die. Others may have imprisoned themselves in a rut of fixed habits of mind. Not Cervantes. He lived by the axiom **Use it or lose it.**

He never stopped learning. He was willing to learn from his failures as well as his successes. He had lots of troubles in life. He never wallowed in self-pity and said, "Why me?" Instead he had the wisdom to say, "What is this problem trying to teach me?"

And, he never lost his enthusiasm. The child of wonder always lived inside the adult. He cared about people and things. He reached out. He took risks. He saw a meaning and glory in life that was larger than his own little needs. He used what he had and not only made the best of it, but he created a masterpiece, for which he will never be forgotten.

The parable of the talents, which Jesus uses in today's gospel tells the same story. God has given each of us spiritual powers so great, "they could move mountains." Jesus says, "Use your soul, or lose it." Permit the powers of your soul to flower and expand every moment of every day. Gandhi was able to fight back the mighty British Empire with his *Ahimsa*, or soul power. With his powers of the soul he brought justice to India.

With our powers of the soul we too can bring justice to others and love to our families and friends. Ultimately, our physical muscles wear out and wear down. But our spiritual muscles never wear out. They just get stronger with the years. It is said that some saints were so full of soul power, that when they died, it seemed as though their souls burst from their bodies. Not only can any of us do it, we have the infinite power of God to make sure we can do it.

All we need to do is **use it!**

Prayer

Christ, our brother, we thank you for the gifts
and talents you have given us. We hope to use
them, lest we lose them. We know that our
physical powers will wear out with time, but we
try to recall that our spiritual powers should
ripen with age and use. Empower us to use our
gifts and talents for the service of love, justice
and mercy. Amen.

Thirty-fourth Sunday of Ordinary Time, Christ the King

Ezekiel 34: 11-12, 15-17
God is a good and caring shepherd.

1 Corinthians 15: 20-26, 28
Jesus is king of creation.

Matthew 25: 31-46
Jesus comes to judge our hearts.

The King of Hearts

Medieval Irish monks tell the story of an old monk who had a vision before his death. It was the middle of the night and moonlight filled his room. The silver moonbeams lit up an angel who was writing on a book of gold. Peace flooded the heart of the monk. Fascinated by the angel, he asked the heavenly being, "What are you writing?" The angel seemed surprised to be asked, but not unwilling to respond. "I am recording the names of those who love the Lord."

"Is my name among them?" asked the monk. The angel scanned the pages and shook his head. "No, I do not find your name here." The answer apparently did not distress the monk. With his usual amiability the monk requested, "Would you mind writing me into that book as a monk that has always loved people?" Quietly, the angel wrote deeply onto the pages of gold. Then the angel disappeared. The following evening a shower of stars filled the monk's room. The angel came again to show the monk the names in the book of gold. Perfect joy shone from his eyes. His name led the list of all those who had loved the Lord.

After his death, the monks read his journal. The very first entry was a quote from St. John's first letter (4: 20): "If anyone says, 'My love is fixed on God,' yet hates his brother, he is a liar. One who has no love for the brother he has seen cannot love the God he has not seen." The monk's own commentary on St. John's lines were, "I sought my soul, but my soul I could not see. I sought my God, but my God eluded me. I sought my brother and sister, and then I found all four."

We know we have a soul, but it is not always easy to sense its existence. We know there is a God, but so often God seems to escape us. We know there are people all around us who need our love and care. In showing them affection and good humored service, we feel our souls come alive and our hearts burn with the presence of God.

This is the feast of Christ the King. Our major reading is about Christ the Judge. Hence the liturgy asks us to contemplate Christ's kingship from the viewpoint of how he will judge us in the end. It is clear that Jesus is the judge of hearts. Or, if you like, the king of hearts. He will not judge us on how bright we are, but on how well we loved. He will not judge us on how rich we became, but on how much wealth of affection we bestowed on those who needed us. Jesus is the king of hearts.

This is judgement day in the liturgy. So we are called to examine our lives. Was I more concerned about obeying laws or about caring for people? Certainly one should obey laws, for we do not want chaos in society or the Church. But if we reduce religion to that, we have missed the point. St. Paul contrasted those who thought salvation was in obeying law and not the greater demand of gospel, which is loving people.

Do I spend my life being scared of God, or use my energies to remove fear and misery from people's lives? The last thing God ever wants us to be is to be scared of Him. God is not interested in frightening us. You may say, "But the Bible says that God is angry with sinners. His wrath will be showered on the bad." That is true, but usually misunderstood. His anger is not the vengeance of a petulant tyrant. His anger is the frustration of a lover who is trying to make us feel good about ourselves. He does not want to intimidate us, but to beg us to wake up and live and love.

If you are having trouble loving God, try loving people. That is the simplest way to find God. Love your neighbor and then you will be pleased to meet the king of hearts.

Prayer

Christ, our king, may we appreciate that we stand under your judgment. We believe you will not judge us on how bright we are, but on how well we loved. You will not evaluate our bank accounts, but you will inspect our hearts. Help us never to reduce religion to anything less than love and care. Help us to believe that when we love our neighbor we will meet you, the true King of hearts. Amen.

The following books are also available from the Religious Education Division of the Wm. C. Brown Company Publishers:

Saints Are People: Church History Through the Saints

Following seven historical periods, this informative reference profiles the lives and works of 31 saints. It gives a biographical sketch of each saint, the significance of his or her work, and a short reflection on the traits the saint exemplified. Written by Rev. Alfred McBride, O.Praem. (#1785, $4.50)

Year of the Lord, Reflections on the Sunday Readings

Whether for individual reflection or informal group enrichment, these new books are for Catholics interested in personal reflection on the three Sunday scripture readings. For each Sunday and major feast of the liturgical year, there is a citation of the readings; summary statements establishing the theme for each reading; a reflection on a general theme suggested by all the readings; and a prayer response. Written by Rev. Alfred McBride, O.Praem. Cycle A (#1847, $6.95); Cycle B (#1848, $6.95); Cycle C (#1849, $6.95)

Written by Mary Jo Tully, each book in the *Shared Faith* series includes a collection of resource readings for the participants. Following each reading are two or three questions that call for the reader's reflection on the material and how it relates to their personal life.

The three books of the *Shared Faith* series are:

Blessed Be

Nine sessions in which adults are urged to discuss the Beatitudes in light of their own experience and belief. (#1822 Blessed Be $3.50)

Church: A Faith-Filled People

Ten sessions focusing on the Church as a community where adults share caring, loving, and belonging through God and each other. (#1823 Church: A Faith-Filled People $3.50)

Psalms: Faith Songs for the Faith-Filled

Eight sessions for adults to increase their appreciation of the Psalms and the enrichment they bring to prayer. (#1824 Psalms: Faith Songs for the Faith-Filled $3.50)

To order, send your name and address, along with the titles and order numbers of the books you want. Please include $1.50 for postage and handling. Payment must accompany order. Send to: Wm. C. Brown Company Publishers
Religious Education Division
P.O. Box 539; 2460 Kerper Blvd.
Dubuque, Iowa 52001